Prestel Museum Guide

State Museum for Art and Design in Nuremberg

Prestel
Munich · London · New York

Neues Museum

State Museum
for Art and Design
in Nuremberg

Address:
Luitpoldstrasse 5
90402 Nuremberg

Entrance at Klarissenplatz

Info line: 0911–24020 10
Press and PR: 0911–24020 41
Administration: 0911–24020 20
Fax: 0911–2402029
Internet: www.nmn.de

Opening hours:
Tues. – Fri. 10 a.m. – 8 p.m.
Sat. – Sun. 10 a.m. – 6 p.m.
Closed on Mondays
(Info valid as of September 2000)

Museum Educational Dept.
Information and booking:
Tel. 0911-24020 36

Digital visitor information
Virtual tours of the Collection and the art section collection catalogue may be viewed on four screens

The Nuremberg Institute of Modern Art
Information and Documentation Centre for Contemporary Art
Archive/Library
Opening times:
Tues. and Fri. 10 a.m. – 4 p.m.
Thurs. 2 p.m. – 7 p.m.
(Info valid as of April 2000)

Restaurant PROUN
Accessed from across the square. Also open outside Musuem opening hours

Buchhandlung Walther König im Neuen Museum (bookshop) and mobilia im Neuen Museum both accessible from Luitpoldstrasse or directly from the Museum.

Museumsinitiative
Freunde und Förderer des Neuen Museums in Nürnberg e.V. (Friends of the Museum)
Luitpoldstrasse 5
90402 Nuremberg
Tel.: 0911–2402020

Contents

A New Museum in Nuremberg 6

The Art Collection 18

The Design Collection 72

Index 126

EIN WERK, EIN

A New Museum in Nuremberg

The fact that, in 2000, a building to house a museum of contemporary art and design has not only been built but an entirely new foundation has been established from scratch, is anything but a matter of course. It is, really, something of a sensation and—in our particular case—a sensation when prerequisites unique to Nuremberg are borne in mind.

Nuremberg—long regarded as a city of culture, once the 'little treasure house of the German Empire' and, for a hundred and fifty years, home to the 'largest museum of German art and culture', the *Germanisches Nationalmuseum*—was the only major German city in which, up until the year 2000, there was no museum for modern and contemporary art, an institution which, especially in Germany, is so exceptionally differentiated and highly developed. It was as if Nuremberg was readily associated with the art and culture of the German past while it remained without an institution dedicated to the art and culture (both national and international) of the present. The municipal *Kunsthalle Nürnberg* was—as far as acquisitorial activities on the museum side were concerned—one of several attempts made since the 1920s to create such an institution, and the only one that was not rapidly abandoned. It remained, however, nothing other than an attempt that foundered at the halfway stage and only later, as a consequence, was it possible to incorporate the holdings of the *Kunsthalle* which, as an exhibition venue for contemporary art was destined to go its own way, into the *Neues Museum*.

One Museum and Two Collections

The *Neues Museum*, which was opened on 15 April, 2000 as the *Staatliches Museum für Kunst und Design in Nürnberg* and which is presented as such for the first time in this guidebook, is an internationally orientated museum for contemporary art and design. To be more precise: its collection focuses on 20th-century art and design since the 1950s and, in due course, on the art and design of present and future decades in the 21st-century (without wanting to reach too far ahead into the future). The holdings united for the first time in the *Neues Museum* have quite distinct origins.

The art collection is the so-called *Sammlung internationaler zeitgenössischer Kunst* of the city of Nuremberg assembled by the *Kunsthalle Nürnberg* since 1967 and on permanent loan to the Free State of Bavaria for the *Neues Museum*, where it now forms the nucleus of the present collection. Additions to this have been made since 1987 and will be further enriched in the future as well by acquisitions made through the *Museumsinitiative*, the *Verein der Freunde und Förderer des Neuen Museums in Nürnberg e.V.* To mark the formal opening of the museum, the collection has been substantially supplemented through a large an important donation, totalling around fifty works, from Marianne and Hansfried Defet—Nuremberg entrepreneurs who, since the 1960s, have played a key role in promoting local interest in contemporary art, not least at their own gallery—and through loans from a number of private collections (René Block, Rolf Ricke et al). It will be continually expanded with acquisitions funded by the State of Bavaria which, in the future, is to assume sole responsibility for this museum. (Since its foundation as an administrative unit on 1 October, 1997, the *Neues Museum* has acquired over forty works and received a total of fifteen in the form of donations).

The spiral staircase

The art collection of the *Neues Museum* thus has its own history and an established structure which evolved subsequently. In its origins it was based on a concept developed by Dietrich Mahlow, the first Director of the *Kunsthalle* in Nuremberg. He foresaw thirty rooms for thirty artists ranging from Oskar Schlemmer, Hans Arp, Josef Albers and other 'father figures' to representatives of what was then the youngest generation, such as Horst Antes and Gerhard Richter. The content of the work was to be broken down into four categories: colour and plane; light and movement; text and image; and New Figuration. In the 1960s and '70s Mahlow's concept was seen as revolutionary, taking the questions raised by the most modern art forms at that time as a means of orientation. Instead of a personal selection by the Director alone, an objective plan was drafted by a committee of international experts from the west and east, based on stylistic and content-related criteria. Since, however, Mahlow left the Kunsthalle in Nuremberg after only four years, the collection never materialised to an extent such that his concept could be clearly seen. Many significant groups of works—such as those by Schlemmer, Arp or Albers—had only been on loan from the artists or their heirs and were withdrawn after Mahlow's departure. It is, nonetheless, thanks to Mahlow that important works from Lajos Kassák to Jiří Kolář were included in the collection and now form a group of works without parallel and, for example, the world's largest collection of pictures by Gabrijel Stupica. Stupica, who emerged as the most important artist of the 20th century in the young state of Slovenia, is however not represented in any other museum in western world. Dietrich Mahlow was, without doubt, one of the few museum directors of his era in Western Europe for whom the art landscape of the continent did not stop at the Iron Curtain.

The four thematic-stylistic categories behind Mahlow's concept were taken on by his successor, Curt Heigl who continued to develop the *Kunstsammlung* in Nuremberg from 1972 to 1988. In addition, for a period of four years, Heigl's acquisitive activities focused on the

Aerial view, 1984

Aerial view, 1999

works of the artist Richard Lindner, who had spent his youth in Nuremberg and who had just been rediscovered in the wake of American Pop Art. As a result, the *Neues Museum* not only possess Lindner's *Telephone* (p. 20), probably the best known and most popular of his paintings, but can also boast one of the largest collections of works by this artist in existence.

From the end of the 1980s, efforts were concentrated on further developing the *Kunstsammlung*, for which the City of Nuremberg had made substantial funds available over a certain period. The aim was to bolster the established strengths of the holding, while simultaneously broadening the scope, so that the relevance and credibility of contemporary artistic activity—in terms of both form and medium—could be experienced fundamentally. Wherever possible, particular emphasis has been placed on the strong conceptual currents in contemporary art and on artists' handling of the most diverse forms of modern media.

The design collection, displayed in the *Neues Museum* alongside the art collection, derives from the very comprehensive holdings of the *Neue Sammlung*, the *Staatliches Museum für angewandte Kunst* in Munich. The selection made by Florian Hufnagl, the director of the *Neue Sammlung*, is based on the period and experimental tendencies reflected in the *Kunstsammlung*, presenting developments in international design from the 1940s and '50s. In the future, the treasures of the *Neue Sammlung* will be on display in two locations: in the *Pinakothek der Moderne* in Munich and in the *Neues Museum* in Nuremberg. Each will present a slightly different cross-section of international design history.

The Nuremberg design collection will, however, remain an independent entity in its own right in the future as well, managed as a 'branch' of the *Neue Sammlung* in Munich. Both the art and the design collection, as different as their histories may be, come together as one logical whole in the *Neues Museum* in Nuremberg.

Nevertheless, art and design are presented separately within the *Neues Museum* with each section having its own floor and its own arrangement while parallels between the two have not been overlooked. Although art and design cannot exist or develop in isolation from one another, nor can it be said that they spring from the same source. More significantly, their presentation in museums has always been subject to utterly different and varying criteria. In the case of a museum of art, the essentially paradoxical principle applies that it removes the work of art from its historical context, presenting it to the viewer in isolation, even if an attempt is made to compensate this with historical information. The actual artistic importance of a work, i.e. what first makes something art, is seen in its timelessness. Only once a work of art has demonstrated its timeless qualities in the face of the most varied evaluations made over several generations, is it recognized as a major work. In a museum of modern and contemporary art this principle is exaggerated by placing works in the most neutral of all environments, namely a white cube, which is nothing but an artificial and isolated room, in which the work of art can lead an utterly autonomous existence, devoid of purpose and, as such, remain timeless.

The very nature of a design object, on the other hand, dictates that it is not devoid of purpose and can never be removed from the historical, evolutionary context in which it was created. This means that a collection of design objects is subject to a general cultural-historical stance, whereas the timeless, artistic value of a work is sought in an art museum.

A chair designed by Gerrit Rietveld placed alongside a painting by Piet Mondrian —to take a hypothetical situation here since both artists belong to an earlier period and, as such, would not be represented in our collections—would automatically reduce the painting to mere documentation of a particular stylistic tendency within the art of the 1920s and would, thereby, hamper the purely aesthetic approach that the museum is striving to open up.

In the case of the *Neues Museum* in Nuremberg which focuses on works from the most recent decades—when more than ever before it is the context that defines art as such—it would cause enormous bewilderment if the two categories were confused. The four motorbikes assembled by Ange Leccia's *Lolita* (p. 63), for example, can communicate through their own particularly aesthetically attuned 'body language' only in the context of works of painting and sculpture. Placed within a museum display that combined art and design, there would be a danger that they would serve as little more than an example of motorbike styling in the early 1990s. The same would also apply to Guillaume Bijl (p. 66) or Christine Hohenbüchler.

The confrontation of art and design in the *Neues Museum* should broaden the viewers' perspective, in the sense of encouraging a more generous definition of art. In no way is it intended for art and design to be subjected exclusively to a cultural-historical viewpoint.

A 'Classic' Art Museum

The apportioning of display space stipulated in the competition terms in 1991 for the *Neues Museum* in Nuremberg, determined that three-quarters of the display area be reserved for items from the permanent collection and only a quarter for temporary exhibitions. This in itself was an important statement: the building was not to be predominantly

Annex and façade

an exhibition venue but rather a museum of the traditional type, with its principle role that of presenting art to the public by drawing on its own collections. Temporary exhibitions were to be purely a supplement to this activity. The designs submitted by Volker Staab underlined this principle even further (either intentionally or unintentionally) by separating the sections for the collections and the exhibition space to such a degree that they could not be brought together. There is no direct physical link. Even if one wanted to, it would never be possible to extend the exhibition space into the areas where the collections are displayed. The situation in many art museums today is such that the permanent collections are being squeezed out more and more, as it is easier to attract the public to temporary exhibitions. The conscious decision not to do this is of central importance: the *Neues Museum* in Nuremberg is designed as a museum with a permanent collection with peripheral, temporary exhibitions and not vice versa.

An Exceptionally Beautiful Building

The Neues Museum has had the privilege of embarking on its work in an extraordinarily beautiful building. It was designed by Volker Staab, who won first prize in the open competition of 1991 and who was then a young, unknown architect from Berlin. For Staab this success has proven to be the beginning of a brilliant career. He has since received commissions for other projects, including an extension to the Maximilianeum in Munich (1992–94) and a building to house the Schäfer Collection in Schweinfurt, which is now nearing completion. After a four-year preparatory period, the *Neues Museum* was constructed between the autumn of 1996 and the end of 1999. It is an exceptional structure in two respects: as an architectural intervention in the Old Town of Nuremberg at an especially sensitive spot, and as an example of architecture that, for all its autonomy, is not allowed to stray from its intended purpose.

The site made available on the southern edge of the Old Town between the Luitpoldstrasse and the Frauentormauer was regarded as highly unsuitable. It was generally considered an ugly, industrial back premises, which one pretended not to notice. As a result of Staab's design, however, this area has been transformed into an attractive focal point to the south of the historic centre. The museum, complete with its own forecourt, was inserted into the surrounding block while carefully respecting the character both of the existing streets and the historical structures. And, precisely as a result of this, no restrictions are imposed on the interior space. The visitor to the Neues Museum encounters a rigorously contemporary structure that is at the same time both accommodating and self-aware, a building possessed of formal structural qualities, but also one that gives art what art needs: clearly defined white spaces without any intruding details, such as are only very rarely to be found in such clarity and purity; and a structure that also embraces, to the great advantage of the museum and its overall impact, a central spiral staircase that itself resembles a piece of sculpture, a series of foyers and an atrium and, above all, a long, sweeping glass façade. This is the architectural element that fully compensates the museum's not especially prominent location. In a single gesture it serves to unite the various components of the interior—the two-storey wing (open along the main façade) housing the collections, the closed cube in the middle and the atrium and old building to the right—and, ultimately, it offers a compelling symbol of accessibility.

Artistic contribution by Rémy Zaugg

During the planning stage there was much talk of the 'openness' with which the museum should be presented. Now one can see its significance looking out from inside the building. The museum opens itself up to anyone standing outside. It allows a view of the space occupied by the collections, of visitors moving up and down the sweeping stairs and along each floor, and of the atrium. The museum opens itself up to anyone inside, too, since there are hardly

Atrium

any rooms which do not have a view to the outside and the square outside appears to be a continuation of the space inside. To whatever degree the 'White Cube' may create a distance between the works in the museum and the everyday world outside and offer art the possibility of an utterly autonomous, timeless existence, devoid of any purpose, the world outside is nevertheless always present in the rooms due to the many different perspectives the visitor has of the town, however attractive or not that view may be.

'One Work, one Human Being, one Perception'

Even if many would dispute the term and sometimes have mixed feelings about it, *Kunst am Bau* (artworks associated with a particular building) is no longer a foreign concept in public buildings commissioned by the State of Bavaria. Accordingly, a portion of the funds allotted for the *Neues Museum* in Nuremberg were reserved for this purpose. But how could the money be allotted so that not only local artists were commissioned—as generally stipulated politically—but that the museum's own requirements as an internationally orientated museum for art and contemporary design could be met? At the same time, a contribution to the subject 'art and architecture' was to be made which should at least be appropriate and perhaps even set a new standard. To be avoided at all costs was a superficial and thus ultimately anti-architectural addition of visual or sculptural elements. That would also have been below expectations and not in keeping with today's artistic possibilities. The first question was then addressed to the architect: where, in his opinion, could art play a convincing role in his design? Just as there was in his scheme a clear distinction between spaces in which works of art and design were to be exhibited and those parts of the building with a purely architectural role (foyers, the spiral

staircase, the atrium, etc.), by the same token, it was argued, there should also be areas in which the desired artistic contribution would be appropriate. The architect's answer was that the best place would be the outer side of the so-called 'Cube', that central section of the building with the space for temporary exhibitions with the foyer and auditorium below. The outer wall of this structure incorporates many technical installations and the cladding is purely to conceal these, thus making it perfect for a work of art in the broadest sense of the term. At the suggestion of the Director of the *Neues Museum*, an invitation to submit designs for this surface was extended to five artists (all of them either already represented in the collection or on the museum's 'wish list' for further acquisitions). A committee, which included the architect himself and representatives of all the institutions connected with the building project (together with an artist and an external museum's director), was then asked to reach a decision, and it was unanimous in selecting the design submitted by Rémy Zaugg. This scheme, while certainly fulfilling the stipulations of the commission, also went beyond these in as far as it extended to other areas of the building. Where the artist was to be given an entirely free hand—on the outer wall of the 'Cube'—his approach was almost that of an architect. He proposed covering the surface with a pale turquoise-toned *stucco lustro* and then inscribing on this background, in a tone only slightly darker, and using the large capital letters that are a hallmark of his work, the phrase: ABER ICH / DIE WELT / ICH SEHE / DICH (But I / the world / I see / you). In addition, Zaugg inscribed other words or phrases on the sandstone cladding of the outer walls of other parts of the building: on the wall of the angular annex that faces the square, above the arcade of the ground-floor restaurant: EIN WERK, EIN MENSCH, EIN WAHRNEHMEN (One work, one human being, one perception); facing the atrium on the rear of the Old Building in which the library of the Institute of Modern Art is situated: EIN HAUS, EIN MENSCH, EINE BIBLIOTHEK (One house, one human being, one library); and on the long façade of the annex, approximately at eye-level for passers-by, he placed the names of famous Nuremberg intellectuals: HANS SACHS—FEUERBACH—VEIT STOSS—HEGEL—ALBRECHT DÜRER. This invocation, which relates the museum to the city's intellectual and cultural history, is also a fond acknowledgement of the tradition of the public museum as an institution, for most museums of fine or applied arts founded and constructed in the 19th century displayed statues and the names of major historic figures associated with their collections in front of the museum.

As a coincidental result of Zaugg's artistic intervention, an inconsistency imposed on the architect was drawn to our attention. For reasons of economy, the rear façade of the Old Building, with its library extension facing the atrium, was not to have the sandstone cladding used for the other façades, but merely to be rendered. In the analysis of the building presented by Rémy Zaugg, this contradiction in architectural logic was pointed out. As a result, the sandstone cladding that the architect had himself wanted to use for this part of the building was added after all as part of the artist's contribution. 'Art and architecture' has really proven itself here in the form of architecturally-related art.

The Collections within the Building

As already mentioned, the art and design collections are presented separately. On the ground floor of the holdings section, composed exclusively of spaces lit by artificial light, is the design collection, whereas on the upper floor, in rooms largely receiving natural light from above, is the art collection. This was an obvious arrangement. In the case of the design collection, its exhibits are displayed on stands or in glass display cases, rendering an element of installation and illumination control necessary. Exhibits in the art collection, on the other hand, benefit from being shown in natural daylight.

The presentation on the ground floor illustrates the historical development of design. The scale of the holdings available to the *Neue Sammlung* enable such a selection. The visitor is led from one room to the next through the design of the 1940s and '50s up through the '90s. The careful way the presentation has been installed is a guarantee that the sequence established for the opening in 2000 will still be kept for many years to come.

The art collection was never assembled on a chronological basis and such a presentation as a historical development would not be suitable. Here, in a sequence of ten rooms, the viewer encounters ten diverse thematic or atmospheric zones, creating a dialogue between a number of fundamental artistic positions. Each arrangement of exhibits can only ever serve as one example among many and the scale and variety of the collection make it unavoidable that a new selection be made at regular intervals. The reader of this guide must, accordingly, be prepared to find that those works on show at the time of his or her visit do not necessarily correspond with those examples described in the following pages.

Further Institutions

In addition to the *Neues Museum*, with its permanent collections, exhibitions and associated events, two further institutions, whose work is connected with that of the museum, are to be found in the same building. The *Institut für moderne Kunst*, founded in 1967 in association with the Nuremberg *Kunsthalle*, is the only centre in Germany for the documentation of international contemporary art. This is housed in the museum's Old Building fronting Luitpoldstrasse, with its library in a purpose-built extension in the museum building. The archive and the library, while being available for use by the curatorial museum staff, are primarily intended for the public and, as such, Nuremberg provides the very best studying facilities in this field. The *Designforum Nürnberg*, financially supported by the Bavarian Ministry of Trade and Industry and largely to advise industries of the region on questions of design, has large working areas and rooms for events on the upper floor of the annex that lies directly opposite the façade.

As such, the *Neues Museum* has the ultimate prerequisites as a place of information and reflection on art and design in the contemporary world —not only for the traditional, art-interested public but also for industry. An internationally renowned bookshop, which carries a specialized selection of publications on contemporary art, architecture and design, a shop specializing in design objects, and a very stylish restaurant complement the palette.

In Conclusion, a Note of Thanks

Like every other aspect of the *Neues Museum* in Nuremberg, this first guide to the building and its collections is a product of successful cooperation.
I should like to express my gratitude to our partners from the *Neue Sammlung*

Upper Floor

in Munich: its Director Florian Hufnagl and his colleagues, in particular Josef Straßer, who provided all the texts concerning the exhibits in the design section. I am especially grateful to my colleagues here at the *Neues Museum*, above all to Thomas Heyden, who not only wrote some of the entries on works in the art section but who also took on the overall editorial management, and to Melitta Kliege and Birgit Suk, both for their own textual contributions and for their input to our discussions regarding the concept of this volume.

Lucius Grisebach

TE
EPHONE

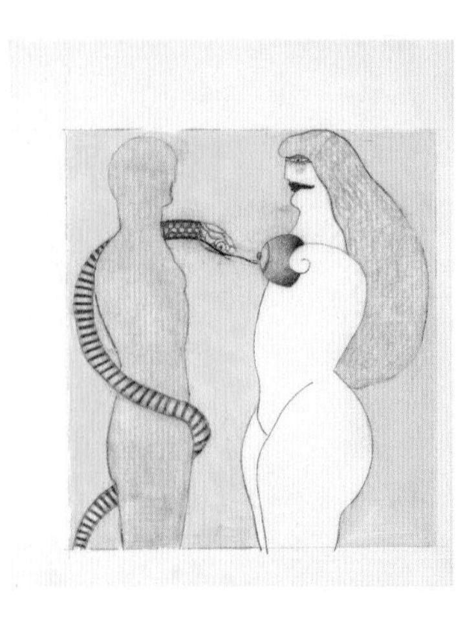

Richard Lindner (1901–78)
Study for *And Eve*, 1970

Crayon on tracing paper, 28.7 x 22.7 cm
On loan from the City of Nuremberg
(where acquired in 1985)

***Uptown*, 1968**

Gouache and graphite on cardboard,
60.7 x 50.2 cm
On loan from the City of Nuremberg
(where acquired in 1985)

***Telephone*, 1966**

Oil on canvas, 178 x 152.5 cm
On loan from the City of Nuremberg
(where acquired in 1975)

Richard Lindner's *Telephone* is the best-known image to be found in the *Neues Museum*. Moreover, this German-American painter is one of the best represented artists in the museum collection, its holdings embracing the *Double Portrait of Ludwig II* of 1974 and a large number of drawings, prints and book illustrations, in addition to this major work of 1966. The Hamburg-born Lindner, both of whose parents were Jewish, came to Nuremberg as a child, attending the city's School of Applied Arts from 1922. Before emigrating in 1933 he had already had some success in his work as a Munich-based illustrator. Initially he moved to Paris, but in 1941 he was able to make his escape to New York where, in 1948, he became an American citizen. For Lindner the artist, encountering the city with the open eyes of a 'tourist', the metropolis offered a superfluity of visual stimuli. 'Every idea that I've explored in my pictures,' he claimed, 'has come from what I've seen here.' In the 1960s Lindner took up the theme of the metropolis, treating its emblematic images and its lonely inhabitants in rigorously composed figure paintings and drawings. The often garish local colour and the 'hard edge' style of the pictorial inventions he derived from the phenomena of popular culture, appeared to situate him close to American Pop Art, from which he nonetheless made an effort to distance himself: 'I admire the Pop Artists [...] But I'm not one of them and I never will be. The real influences on my work have been Giotto and Piero della Francesca [...].' Lindner remained an artist deeply indebted to the European tradition, one whose work is unimaginable without the example of Fernand Léger, Oskar Schlemmer or Balthus. *Telephone* is one of the most succinct of Lindner's metropolitan

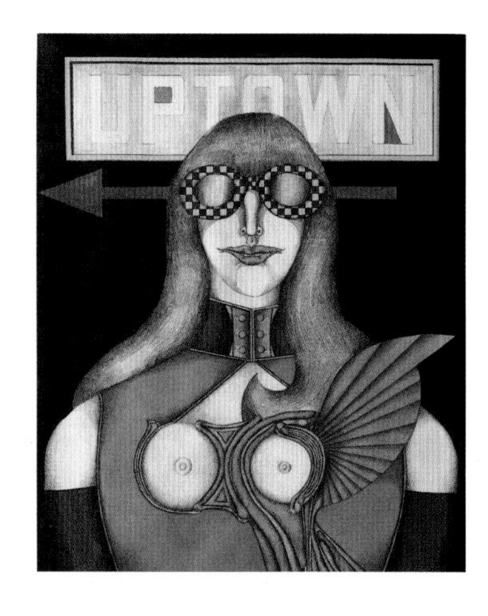

images. In a telephone booth a woman and a man stand back to back. Their figures appear rigid, resembling automata rather than individuals. Their clothes have the simultaneously defensive and aggressive character of suits of armour, rendering them untouchable. The only cursorily modelled bodies seem almost two-dimensional. Their firmly outlined, emphatically stylized forms tend towards rectilinearity and geometry: the woman's breast forms an almost perfect circle while, on the man's overcoat, a yellow seam on the sleeve runs exactly parallel with the central door frame and the four buttons mark out an exact square. Lindner draws the viewer's attention to the emphatically reduced pictorial space in showing his figures partially in front of and partially behind the red cabin walls that frame them. The relationship between man and woman, which here appears to be lapsing into extreme isolation, was one of the central themes of Lindner's work. In his drawn study for the painting *And Eve* the darting tongue of a phallic snake caresses the breast of Eve, which here symbolizes the apple of the Original Sin. Similarly, the figure in *Uptown* displays her naked breasts like fetishes. Beneath the masks of the metropolis, Lindner's pictorial universe lays bare the lusts, obsessions and anxieties of its inhabitants. (TH)

Jiří Kolář (born 1914)
***Hommage à Christian Morgenstern,* 1965/66**

I: Chiasmage: red sealing wax, paper and thread on hardboard, 200 x 120 cm
II: Bridge of a musical instrument: red sealing wax and paper on wood, 83.5 x 69.5 x 10.5 cm
II: Apple: red sealing wax and paper on polystyrene, dia. 50 cm
On loan from the City of Nuremberg (where acquired in 1971)

***Great Dead Language,* 1965**

Printed paper on hardboard, 200 x 120 cm
On loan from the City of Nuremberg (where acquired in 1971)

The *Neues Museum* possesses a great many works by Jiří Kolář from the 1960s, including his *Diary* of 1968. In no other German museum is it possible to study so thoroughly the work of this Czech artist, who has established his own territory on the border between literature and visual art. Kolář took the art of collage, as featured in the work of the Cubists, the Futurists and the Dadaists, and developed it in a bewildering variety of directions. Depending on the materials and techniques employed in each case, he would call the resulting work a *rollage*, a *prollage*, a *chiasmage* and so on. The *Great Dead Language* of 1965 is an early example of *chiasmage*, a term derived from *chiasmus*, a concept from the art of rhetoric indicating the repetition of a phrase or clause with inverted word order. Through the suffix *-age*, Kolář alludes to the French notion of *collage*. The artist's *chiasmages* consist of countless small fragments of texts and illustrations that are then very carefully reconstructed in a variety of arrangements. These may often be found to resemble those natural structures that

especially fascinated Kolář: the feathers of birds' wings, fish-scales, the leaves carpeting the ground in autumn.

For the *Great Dead Language* the artist selected as his 'raw material' paper with notations for old church hymns and the text of a Czech edition of the Bible. The upright picture format resembles a segment from a larger structure of concentric circles that seem as if they may well continue into infinity. Its core consists of musical notes surrounded by a halo of fragments of text printed in black and red. Nowhere does the eye find a place at which to rest. It seeks to follow the individual lines, loses track of these, is seized by the circular movement and sucked into its centre or is flung out again as if with centrifugal force. It remains uncertain as to whether the structure is expanding or contracting. The centre of the composition thus stands at both its beginning and its end. This ambivalence also characterizes the thematic aspect of the work. The musical compositions and the texts, which were once made up of notes and words, have not survived the process of fragmentation. Both text and music thus merge into the picture. This explains the title of this work. At the same time, however, the piece could be perceived as presenting a work in which the processes of coming into being, in as far as both text and music are still in the process of becoming. It is as if we are confronted with the state of creative frenzy, in which all imaginable sentences and melodies await only the acts of formulation and composition. In the case of the *Hommage à Christian Morgenstern* Kolář made use of old manuscripts. He said: 'I enjoy working with hand-written texts and with paper on which time has left its mark [...].' Here a rectangular surface, in addition to objects in the form of the bridge of a stringed instrument and an apple are entirely covered with the smallest scraps of paper. Red sealing wax is used to place marks within the otherwise homogeneous structure. This tripartite work was shown in 1968 at the exhibition 'documenta IV' in Kassel. Kolář dedicated it to Christian Morgenstern, of whom he declared: 'He was one of the first great poets [...].' (TH)

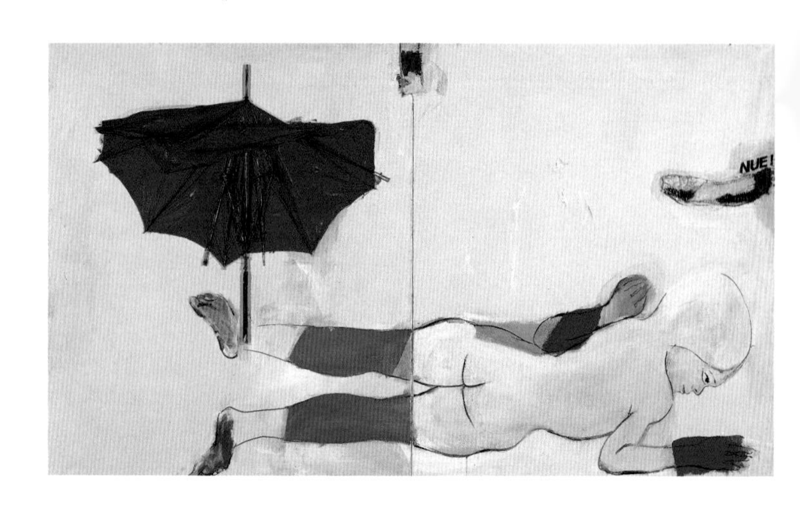

Tadeusz Kantor (1915–90)
***Emballage, Objects, Figures, No. III,* 1968**

Distemper and red umbrella on canvas,
130 x 220 cm
On loan from the City of Nuremberg
(where acquired in 1968)

Tadeusz Kantor, a Pole whose work effectively bridges the realm of the theatrical and the visual, had many connections with Nuremberg. Kantor had good friends in the city, the happenings he initiated and the first performances of his theatre pieces took place in Nuremberg, and in 1968 Dietrich Mahlow, the first Director of the Nuremberg *Kunsthalle*, made the film *Kantor ist da* [Kantor's here]. It was in connection with this project that Kantor made his *Emballage, Objects, Figures, No. III.* During the second half of the 1960s Kantor often united a painted human figure and a real umbrella in his work. Here we find the same need to break out of the illusionism of the easel painting that led the American artist Robert Rauschenberg to make his 'Combine Paintings'. Kantor leaves (real) object and (painted) figure without any anecdotal connection. Here, the reclining female figure remains 'naked' — and, indeed, the French word *nue* [naked] appears as an element of collage. At the same time, the umbrella is possessed of a life of its own that is as puzzling as it is ambivalent, and that the artist once described as follows: 'The umbrella is a curious metaphorical form of *emballage*, it represents a sort of "packaging" for many aspects of human life, it harbours poetry, uselessness, perplexity, defencelessness, unselfishness, hope and risibility.' The concept of the *emballage* [packaging] was central to Kantor's thinking and his work. Certain things are by their very nature already *emballages*, in that they shelter and hide other things. Among these are bags, rucksacks, clothes, envelopes and packages; and all of these play a special role in Kantor's work. Through the act of wrapping things and people in a form of artistic 'ritual', the artist draws attention to their existence. At the same time, he directs particular attention to the theme of the human: 'The act of wrapping something embraces within itself a very human passion and a very human need for preservation, separation, survival and continuation.' With his understanding of the *emballage* as a form of action and ceremonial, Kantor broke through the conventional bounds of the visual arts. (TH)

Gabrijel Stupica (1913–90)
***The Painter and his Model*, 1974**

Distemper and mixed media on wood,
239 x 146 cm
On loan from the City of Nuremberg
(where acquired in 1975)

The painter Gabrijel Stupica, a Slovene, was among the most internationally famous representatives of modern art in the former Yugoslavia. His work is exceptionally well represented in the *Neues Museum*, the collection containing several large-format paintings. Stupica returns repeatedly to the same few themes. *The Painter and his Model* addresses a motif that Stupica treated in many different guises. The figure of the painter, his palette held in his left hand, is to be understood as the artist's self-portrait. It seems to hover almost clumsily in mid-air. The right hand reaches down towards a young girl who herself appears to reach out for physical contact. The two seem to be linked through a tender intimacy. In an earlier version of the same subject, painted in 1956, the girl is identified in the title as the painter's daughter. But there, and even more so in the picture of 1974, an autobiographical reading of the child is not the only possible one. She also embodies the artist's Muse.

The motif itself and the childlike and naive style of presentation are mutually enlightening. Representatives of Modernism were always searching for untapped reservoirs of unadulterated expression. They found these in the work of the socalled 'primitives', of the mentally disturbed, and of children. In many respects, Stupica's work resembles the *art brut* of the French artist Jean Dubuffet, who also drew inspiration from the creativity of children. In comparison with Dubuffet, however, Stupica appears incomparably more tender and poetic. There is a lucidity about the whiteness of his picture space. Stupica spoke of '[...] a would-be world, the obverse image of fear, a white rarefied atmosphere in which we feel secure.' Colour has been applied with refreshing economy. The graphic linearity and painterly moment are balanced exactly. Collage elements permit the outside world a brief glimpse into a sphere that is essentially private. (TH)

Wolf Vostell (1932–98)
***Novillada*, 1960 / 61**

Paper on chipboard, 96.5 x 80 cm
On loan from the City of Nuremberg
(where acquired in 1968)

It could be a detail from a poster in Spain; announcements of bull fights stuck on top of one another and haphazardly torn by those passing by. Fragments of images and text interpenetrate. At the centre of the phrases and words we see the word *Novillada*, the picture's title, a term meaning a fight with young bulls. But what at first appears to be a 'found object' is in fact a deliberate artistic act. Vostell used to speak of the process of *dé-coll/age*. By this he certainly did not intend to evoke only a destructive counterpart to the *collages* of the Cubists and the Dadaists. At the same time he was aiming at much more than were the *affichistes* of *Nouveau Réalisme*, who also worked with haphazardly torn posters. Vostell claimed 'I'm concerned with *dé-coll/age* as a process, as a new theory of art [...].' In 1954 he discovered the word used in the French newsaper *Le Figaro*, in the headline of an article recounting the crash of an aeroplane only shortly after take-off (*décollage*). For Vostell, this concept conveyed the 'ambivalence of events or procedures in the twentieth century.' In a narrower sense he used the term to indicate all those technical processes and forms of action that he had himself developed in order to merge the most diverse levels of reality. The torn posters of the '50s and early '60s were, accordingly, models for the artistic strategies — notably the merging of varieties of media and content — that Vostell adopted, from 1962, when he joined the Fluxus movement. (TH)

Manolo Millares (1926–73)
***Cuadro (Homúnculo)*, 1966**

Oil on sacking, 133 x 100 cm
On loan from the City of Nuremberg
(where acquired in 1966)

The Spanish artist Manolo Millares worked with sacking from the mid-1950s. Earlier, the Italian Alberto Burri had discovered sacking as a 'poor' material for use in art, hence the term *arte povera*. Millares tore the rough cloth and made holes in it; he tangled and wound it. He then mounted what was effectively a sacking relief on a support made of the same material. Millares's style of painting was equally expressive and gestural. He used black and white to create a dramatic contrast. The brown of the cloth and sparingly applied elements of lettering also contributed to the effect. From 1956 Millares called many of his works simply *Cuadro* [Picture]. The additional title used here, *Homúnculo*, [Homunculus], emphasises a detected proximity to the figurative and recalls maltreated human bodies. Millares translated American Abstract Expressionism into a European composition, enriching it with sculptural values. This sombre, existential pathos located Millares within the tradition of Spanish art. Alongside Antoni Tàpies (a Catalan) and Antonio Saura, Millares was one of the true innovators in Spanish art in the era of Franco. (TH)

Otto Piene (born 1928)
***Red Night – Dark Flower*, 1963 / 64**

Oil, rust and fire on canvas, 170.5 x 121 cm
On loan from the City of Nuremberg
(where acquired in 1967)

On a red-painted canvas five deep black circular stains have formed through direct contact with a flame. Rust has formed around the looming traces of the fire, its *sfumato* effect mediating between black and red. In this process of 'painting with fire', the presence of the flame is far more immediate than in any illusionistic image of a conflagration. The primeval violence of fire is present in the very microstructure of the burnt surface. The heat appears as if stored up within the saturated red. In 1963 Piene spoke of the 'possibility of letting painting simply happen like growth in nature, as a controlled, autonomous process.' The 'zero point' back to which the 'Zero' artists of the 1950s – Otto Piene and Heinz Mack – endeavoured to take art was also intended as the point of departure for a new level of sensitivity. The 'Zero' artists were preoccupied with the phenomena of light, space and movement. Starting with the grid structures of his first 'Zero years', Piene later added traces of smoke to his images and he eventually started to work with fire. In the early 1960s the French artist Yves Klein, who was close to the 'Zero' group, also produced a series of fire pictures. (TH)

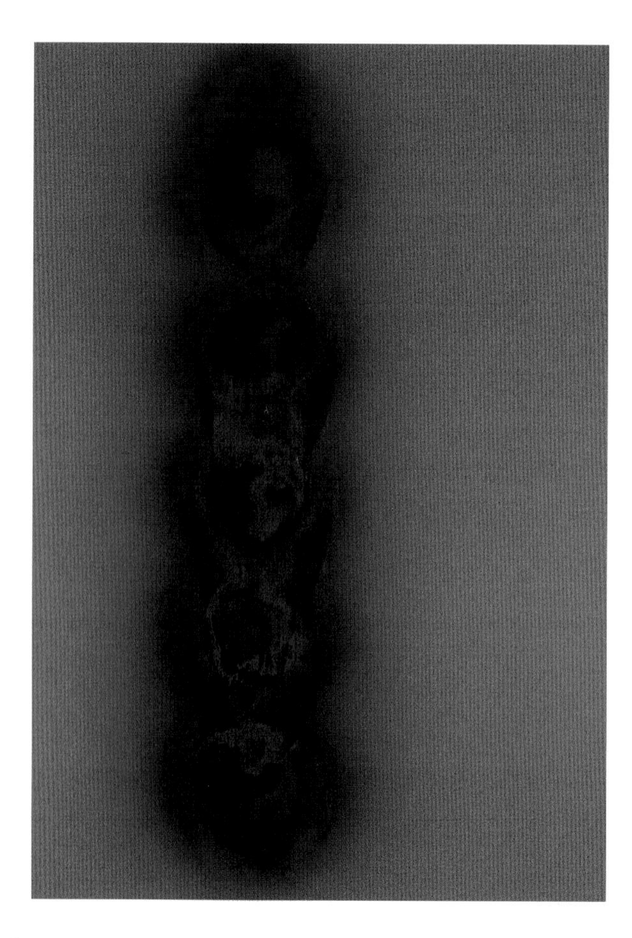

Jan Schoonhoven (1914–94)
***R 74–19*, 1974**

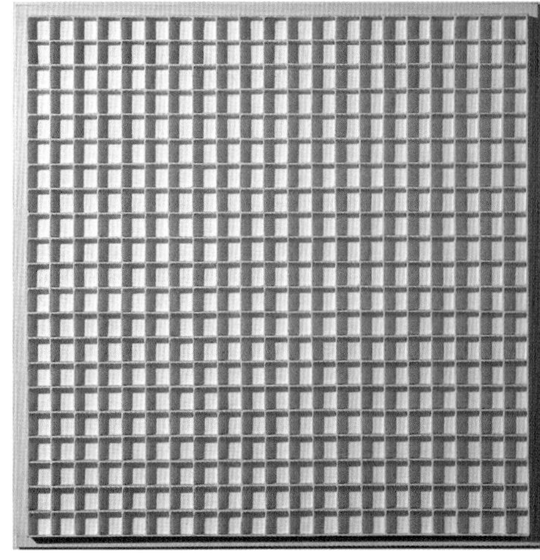

White housepaint, paper and cardboard on wood, 90 x 90 cm
On loan from the City of Nuremberg (acquired in 1986)

A white square is divided into 21 by 21 shallow relief-planes. The rigour of the structure draws the viewer's attention to the light effects that alter according to the illusion and the position of the spectator. The result is a wealth of chiaroscuro nuances, the delicacy and fugacity of which contrasts strangely with the rigidity of the grid. Schoonhoven's relief belongs within the tradition of Concrete Art, which rejects every form of illusion. The expressive values of colour and form here reach almost to an absolute minimum, while the 'figurative' quality of this work simultaneously attains an extreme of reductionism in the form of monochrome white. As a result of the grid structure, the picture is in effect identical with itself, for the internal connections within the picture plane are derived from its limitations, just as the picture plane itself is to be understood as the outcome of its inner structure. Yet, light and shadow, introduced by way of the shallow relief, break open the hermetic quality of the monochrome grid and transform it into an object of the elementary experience of seeing.

Much then depends on the active engagement of the spectator. This is also true as regards the grid, with its slight irregularities in the relief. These were something that the artist positively sought: 'If I have a rectangle and I glue material on to it so as to create a relief, then there has to be [...] a touch of poetry to it. Yes, so that one could say it is "alive". Otherwise I might just as well have it made in a factory.'

Although Schoonhoven, a Dutchman, studied art in The Hague from 1930 to 1934, he earned his living as an official working for the Netherlands postal service from the end of the Second World War until his retirement. He made his first reliefs in the mid-1950s. In 1960, together with the artists Armando, Jan Henderikse and Henk Peeters, Schoonhoven founded the group 'Nul' [Nought] which was itself an offshoot of the Dutch group of Informal artists. In many respects, 'Nul' was a parallel development to the 'Zero' group in Germany. Decisive in both cases was the radical rejection of the subjectivity of Informal Art, which had itself also influenced Schoonhoven in the 1950s. 1960 signified a turning point in his work and one especially clearly documented in his reliefs. They lost their former, often organic animation while acquiring greater structural stability. The use of white signalled the indeterminate emptiness of a new beginning and also stood for the sum of all colours in unrefracted light. Schoonhoven had found his 'subject' and he was to explore it in its most subtle variations over the following years. (TH)

Bridget Riley (born 1931)
***High Sky 2*, 1992**

Oil on canvas, 165 x 228 cm
Gift from Dr. Karl Gerhard Schmidt to the Museumsinitiative e.V., 1992

The English painter Bridget Riley is always engaged in a search for colour. To this end, she draws on the colourist tradition in Western painting, but equally on the impressions that she gathers during her travels around the world. Her palette hints at the natural world without directly imitating it. The title of this work, *High Sky*, suggests a latent relationship to nature. The artist tames the dazzling profusion of colours (such as has been found in her work since the early 1980s) into an almost 'musical', geometrical structure. Riley has justified her high regard for formal discipline in saying: 'If limits are no longer imposed on the modern artist, this only means that he has the freedom to set his own limits [...].' In 1986 she started to move away from work incorporating vertical stripes (which are still, however, to be found in another picture by her in the collection of the *Neues Museum, Summer's Field*, of 1982), and started to favour diagonal structures.

In *High Sky 2*, painted in 1992, vertical and diagonal stripes overlap each other, the latter only half the width of the former. As a result of an illusion of reiterated 'border crossings', the system loses its strictness. As many as four planar segments of the same colour may be connected; and, through the merging of colours from neighbouring vertical stripes, the diagonals are brought out more strongly. The result is a tissue of colour that seems to flicker before our eyes. The distribution of colours does not follow a strict rule but nor is it entirely accidental. However anti-compositionally Riley plans out the picture plane through its organization into stripes of notionally equal value, she still engages in true composition when it is a question of arranging the colours themselves. Bridget Riley's paintings are exceptionally appropriate objects for that 'joy in seeing' of which the artist speaks. (TH)

Gotthard Graubner (born 1930)
Colour-Space Body — Untitled, 1977

Acrylic on nettle on foam-rubber
200 x 200 cm
Gift of Marianne and Hansfried Defet

'Colour is subject enough for me': this is Gotthard Graubner's artistic creed. In his 'Colour-Space Bodies' the painter fully explores the spatial dimension of colour. As a support he uses canvases that curve gently over a padding made of synthetic cotton wool. In contrast to traditional two-dimensional picture surfaces, which can be viewed and understood as a segment from a larger whole, Graubner's colour 'cushions' exist within a world of their own. The 'Colour-Space Bodies' bestow on colour a sensual body mass that appears to 'breathe'. Colour may be said to materialize. At the same time, the support itself becomes dematerialized. Standing in front of Graubner's 'Colour-Space Bodies', the viewer's experience is two-fold. As Graubner says: '[...] in these Colour-Spaces [viewers] lose themselves, but at the same time [...] they can also find themselves [...]. The two poles are an extremly important aspect. To "finding oneself" there may also be a "loosing oneself".'(TH)

Günter Fruhtrunk (1923–82)
***Oppositional Joy*, 1981**

Acrylic and casein on canvas, 166.5 x 211.5 cm
On loan from the City of Nuremberg
(where acquired in 1990 as a bequest from the estate of Günter Fruhtrunk and Hiltrud Fruhtrunk-Steffens)

In the European tradition of Geometric Abstraction, the painting of Günter Fruhtrunk occupies a special place. Although it clearly has its origins in this tradition (Fruhtrunk went to France in the early 1950s, worked there alongside Fernand Léger and Hans Arp and took a great interest in the paintings of Auguste Herbin and others). In the late 1950s and early 1960s, however, a radical change was apparent in Fruhtrunk's approach: the traditional, Constructivist principle of a balanced composition created out of individual, geometrically defined forms (circles, rectangles, lines) on or within the plane of the easel picture was relinquished in favour of an apparently dynamic pictorial structure made out of various parallel broad colour stripes running across the entire surface of the work. Here, the difference between form and surface (between 'figure' and 'ground') — a fundamental problem for all painters operating with elementary forms — was removed. The most characteristic works of this sort to be made by Fruhtrunk are those with series of juxtaposed diagonal stripes. With such works, Fruhtrunk comes near to the exponents of American Hard Edge Painting, who were similarly more concerned with structure than with composition in the traditional sense. In 1958 (in a letter to the artist Max Bill) Fruhtrunk himself defined his aim as 'a spiritual penetration of colour and rhythm'. The *Neues Museum* collection has works from various phases of Fruhtrunk's development, starting in the 1950s. The picture illustrated here, a work of 1981, is the last of these, and has been selected because it may be seen as the most radical in its simplification. (LG)

Gerhard von Graevenitz (1934–83)
***Seven Ovals, White on Black*, 1969**

Kinetic object, wood, dia. 182 cm, depth 17.6 cm; on loan from the City of Nuremberg (where acquired in 1971)

The kinetic objects that Graevenitz made from 1961 evolved from his own previous experiments with more conventional easel painting. They are the result of a process that was intended to free the picture from its close connection to its maker. The work of art, according to Graevenitz, should no longer express the sentiments and feelings of the artist but, rather, lead a life of its own grounded in clearly recognizable principles of structure and form. Towards the end of the 1950s, accordingly, paintings gave way to white structural reliefs, and these in turn evolved into varieties of kinetic objects. The element of movement, which introduced a high degree of chance into the equation, was thus added to the clearly defined principles of structure and form. Here, the black plane as a whole turns within its own frame while, on the black surface, the white oval shapes also turn on their own axes. The energy contained within the work thus issues in an endless series of formal arrangements. The process is powered by a seemingly old-fashioned mechanism driven by electronic motors and belts. Gravenitz commented: ‘My work occupies a place somewhere between research and play. I'm primarily interested in systems that relate to visual perception. I don't use materials and techniques passed down through the centuries, but new, everyday ones.’ (LG)

Dora Maurer (born 1937)
***Provisional Screen Quasi-Picture,* 1983/84**

Acrylic on chipboard in three parts,
150 x 360 cm
On loan from the City of Nuremberg
(where acquired in 1993)

The Hungarian artist Dora Maurer has used the term 'quasi-picture' (*Quasi-Bild*) to designate one of the picture types that she has evolved. While this sort of work appears to have a connection with the tradition of the painted easel picture, it nonetheless departs from it in many respects. The starting point of all Maurer's 'quasi-pictures' is a system described as follows by the artist: 'The system consists of a gradual displacement of four double-layered rectangles (with sides in the proportions 4:5) into a grid-net of 10 by 10 units. The rectangles each embrace 25 units and are enclosed by coloured lines or marked with parallel diagonal lines. The lower layer of the rectangle is picked out with warm tones and it slides, now horizontally, now vertically, from corner to corner; the upper layer has cold colours and is shifted diagonally. Through this movement there come about multifarious overlapping formations.' This system was first elaborated by Dora Maurer in a series of 78 gouaches. One of the two versions of this series is to be found in the collection of the *Neues Museum*. Each of the individual 'quasi-pictures' is a segment from this very complex structure of 'multifarious overlapping formations'. They are not to be understood as compositions in the traditional sense, in which the position of individual forms arises from its relationship to the overall framework; rather, they are images with their outer limits derived from an inner structure that itself forms part of the overall system. While the painting illustrated here appears with a rectangular outline, its truly determining structural elements are its horizontal, vertical and diagonal coloured stripes. The picture owes its inner construction to its alignment and it thus stands with its outline positioned diagonally in relation to the wall. (LG)

Georg Karl Pfahler (born 1926)
Espan No. 43, 1980

Acrylic on canvas, 200 x 200 cm
On loan from the City of Nuremberg (where acquired in 1991 as a gift from the artist)

Of all the German painters of Georg Karl Pfahler's generation, he is probably the one for whom the European tradition of Geometric Abstraction is linked most intensively and autonomously with the principal elements of American Color Field Painting. Pfahler's pictorial compositions are made up of clear geometric forms, yet there is no sense of a compulsion to achieve geometric consistency such as characterizes European Concrete Art. The formal structures in Pfahler's pictures are freely devised, subject only to the logic of the picture surface. Especially significant is an emphatically graphic effect. Pfahler's pictorial language, which evolved its characteristic vocabulary of forms and luminous colours at the end of the 1950s, was symbolic of the new freedom associated with the coming decade, in which artists hoped to be able to express themselves in a universally comprehensible language and without any connection to a national stylistic tradition. Pfahler's paintings are produced in series, each dominated by particular arrangements of form and colour. In the case of the series 'Espan', the title derives from the Spanish word for Spain, *España*, in allusion to a trip to that country in 1975. This is counted as the most extensive of Pfahler's series, and it has in fact been continued, in various phases, until today. The *Neues Museum* has another picture from this group, *Espan No. 69A*, painted in 1989. (LG)

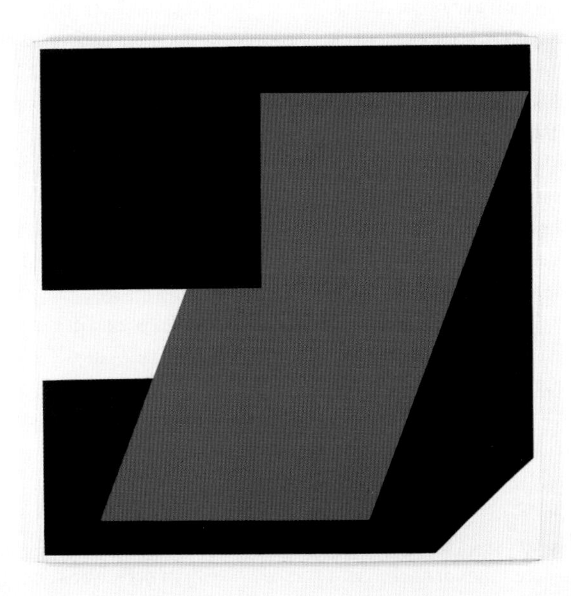

Egon Eppich (1927–82)
***Untitled*, c 1980**

Acrylic on canvas, 107 x 96.5 cm
On loan from the City of Nuremberg
(acquired 1994 as a gift from the artist's estate)

The influence of the German artist Egon Eppich has sadly remained limited to the Nuremberg area, and he is an artist that we have now to re-discover. In addition to his work as a painter – much of it, from the 1960s to 1980, to be found in the collection of the *Neues Museum* – Eppich was an assiduous print-maker and he also produced sculptural and in particular architectural work. Throughout his career, he engaged in a continuous dialogue with the evolution of Concrete Art, and his works can be understood as an autonomous contribution to this markedly international artistic tendency.

In his painting Egon Eppich passed through most of the significant developments of the 1960s and '70s. His concrete formal vocabularly developed gradually from the flattening of simplified and objective elements. In a certain sense, Eppich's non-objective pictures are also informed by the memory of landscape images. At the end of the 1960s important inspiration was derived from the diversely overlapping grid structures evolved by the exponents of Op Art. Out of these, Eppich created autonomous compositions of enormous decorative power. While the work of many adherents of the Op Art of Victor Vasarely or Bridget Riley remained limited to mere optical illusions, that of Egon Eppich achieved a pictorial structure that permitted the emergence of both a planar rhythm with complex spatial effects and the free play of colour. The painting illustrated here, assumed to date from around 1980, is one of a small group of pictures in which a number of grey rectangles are placed in relation to each other within a dove-coloured plane. Their arrangement is based not in a geometrical planar logic. Viewed in terms of the plane, it relates to a well-balanced relation between form and space and, in terms of space, to a balance in which there is no longer any distinction between figure and ground. (LG)

ulije Knifer (born 1924)
Meander 3 DY XI – XII, 1998

Acrylic on canvas, in two parts, 190 x 320 cm
On loan from the City of Nuremberg
(where acquired in 1991)

The Croatian Julije Knifer belongs to a generation of avant-garde artists from the former Yugoslavia that came together in 1959 to found the Zagreb-based group 'Gorgona'. Knifer is virtually the only member to have achieved an international reputation. 'Gorgona' continued until 1966 and was regarded as the union of those artists who were concerned with new media and new creative principles, not unlike the 'Zero' group in Düsseldorf or 'Nul' in Holland. The 'Gorgona' artists never sought to maintain a single shared style. The group published its own journal and mounted exhibitions in its own gallery, 'Studio G'. In addition to the work of 'Gorgona' members, this also showed that of important representatives of the Western European avant-garde such as Piero Dorazio, Piero Manzoni or François Morellet. This made the Zagreb of this period into one of the most outstanding art centres in Communist Eastern Europe.

Knifer's unmistakable 'trademark' is the meander. As early as 1960 the artist was already only using this motif in his pictorial compositions, and only in black and white. Concentration on one basic form and its variations allows the greatest distinctions to be drawn. Every alteration is extremely small, but thereby all the greater in significance. Among the artists of Knifer's generation, there are some in whose work one encounters the same phenomenon. They mark out for themselves a framework, within which their relationship to a particular issue may be ever more precisely specified (for example, the Pole Roman Opałka, whose number pictures started in 1965 on the basis of an unshakable principle and are intended to come to an end only with the artist's death).
In his meander, Knifer has secured a 'meditative sign', in relation to which, similar to minute changes in a heartbeat, even the slightest shift (for example the diverse breadth of the white 'intermediate space' between the black 'forms') has enormous impact. While remaining loyal to the easel picture, Knifer has nonetheless freed it from every connection with illusion or expression and has thus bestowed on it a measure of autonomy. (LG)

François Morellet (born 1926)
***1 carré et sa diagonale, 1/4 de cercle et son rayon (One Square and its Diagonal, One Quadrant of a Circle and its Radius)*, 1985**

Blue neon tubes, electric cable and transformer, 212 x 300 x 150 cm
On loan from the City of Nuremberg (where acquired in 1992)

The *Manifesto of Concrete Art* published in 1930 by Theo van Doesburg, a follower and collaborator of Piet Mondrian, supplied all the grounds for an art that would not proceed by constructing images individually but according to scientifically controllable rules, and that would be an intellectual invention achieved with all precision. By this means Van Doesburg sought to 'realize clarity'. François Morellet is a member of the next generation of artists, those who were able to build on these foundations but at the same time to play with what they had made possible.

On one hand Morellet dedicated himself to exploring the interplay of order and chance. He evolved concepts in which clearly formulated handicaps allowed an element of the accidental to come into play and to impinge on the paintings or sculptures that resulted. What one tends to see in such works as the result of artistic deliberation has in fact come about 'by chance'. On the other hand, he exploited the systematic approach of Concrete Art. The definition supplied in the title of the work illustrated here is of the utmost clarity. *One Square and its Diagonal, One Quadrant of a Circle and its Radius*. Its realization, however, infringes the rules. The geometrical configuration consists in part of luminous neon tubes (one side of the square and the diagonal folded down on to the floor), and in part of the subsidiary element of the cables (the quadrant of a circle and — re-located to one side — its radius). The rules, Morellet seems to be telling us, do not have to be followed absolutely, one can apply them creatively. (LG)

Leon Polk Smith (1906–96)
***Green – Two Black Edges*, 1984**

Acrylic on canvas, wood, 188 x 432 cm
On loan from the City of Nuremberg
(where acquired in 1990)

The American artist Leon Polk Smith has himself characterized his painting as a combination of the ideas of Piet Mondrian and Hans Arp, seeing its essential aim to be 'the creation of space'. As the offspring of a farming family from Oklahoma with Native American ancestors, Leon Polk Smith came late to painting. In New York, from the late 1930s to the 1950s, he developed as an artist through his engagement with the varieties of Abstraction that made their way to America from Europe. From Mondrian's work he drew the rigorous intellectual approach that permitted only clearly defined pictorial means, while from Hans Arp he learnt that the artist might adopt a playfully free approach to form. Smith's 'Correspondence Pieces', made in the 1950s, treat the interrelation of forces between two colour planes within the rectangular picture format. His 'Conversation Pieces' from the 1960s and '70s relocate this interrelation beyond the boundaries of the picture format in as far as many pictures are combined to create a composition. The individual picture opens up a space around itself. Both of these series represent important stages in the development of American Color Field Painting.

Within the scope of American painting Smith and Ellsworth Kelly are – in many respects – working in the same field, although their origins and objectives are different. Kelly's early works were influenced by the coloured surface areas in Henri Matisse's paintings and not by surface systematics and the *weltanschauung* upheld by Mondrian.

Green – Two Black Edges is a late work made when the artist was nearly 80. Here it is evident that he drew on rich and varied experience in dealing with planes in relation to space. With its two black borders extending beyond the ostensible limits of the picture, it reaches out to the wall and draws this into its own space. Paintings of this sort were to some degree rehearsed in the large collages made in the 1980s, in which Smith worked with corresponding arrangements of coloured papers and black lines drawn on a white ground.

(LG)

Joseph Beuys (1921–86)
***Sweeping Out*, 1972 / 85**

Glass display case, street rubbish, broom, numerous plastic bags (Schellmann 40), 202 x 233 x 61.5 cm
On loan from a private collection

Crumpled and torn bits of paper, old drink cans, tattered plastic bags, empty cigarette packets, matches, dog-ends and dust – rubbish from the street has been heaped, sloping up towards the rear, in a glass display case. On top of it lies a street cleaner's broom with red bristles. The contents of this case were part of the exhibition 'Sweeping Out', which opened on the evening of 1 May 1972 at the Galerie René Block in West Berlin. The pieces displayed in the exhibition had formed part of his 'Aktion' of the same name, which had taken place on the morning of the same day, unseen by the public, in the Karl-Marx-Platz in the Neukölln district of the city. Armed with broom and shovel and with plastic bags in which to put the rubbish collected, Beuys swept the square with two of his students, the West African El Loko and the Korean Hiroshi Hirosi, directly after a street demonstration against the official May Day Celebrations organised by the German Alliance of Trade Unions. The rubbish collected was brought in the plastic bags to a Volkswagen bus that was standing at the ready, and, at the end of the happening, this was driven to the gallery. There, the rubbish was shaken out along a wall, the empty plastic bags added and the broom laid diagonally across the top of the heap of sweepings. The display case of 1985 preserves this situation.

The carrier bags in which the rubbish was collected are among Beuys's multiples. A year earlier, in 1971, they had been produced, in an edition of 10,000, for a street happening in Cologne. They contain diagrams that compare two forms of social organisation and prompt consideration of how 'the dictatorship of the Party may be overcome'. Beuys distributed these to passers-by in order to provoke them into discussion. He pursued this goal in the exhibition itself, where both the relics of the 'Aktion' and the political significance of the date provided the starting point for debate. The display case itself provides a graphic exposition of the ideas Beuys then sought to convey. As if by chance, the two key words stare out from the rubbish that surrounds them: a 'yes' to democracy and a 'no' to the dictatorship of the Party. (MK)

George Maciunas (1931–78)
***One Year*, 1972**

Food packaging on wood, 210 x 350 x 12 cm
On loan from a private collection

Orange juice, eggs or cottage cheese were once inside the packaging that George Maciunas used to create this wall object, a piece that is rather atypical for the work and concerns of this artist, who came to the USA via Germany. The question as to whether Maciunas, who trained as a designer, really was an artist has been frequently asked. As founder of the Neo-Dadaist Fluxus movement, he produced manifestos, devised diagrams, organised events and festivals, published a Fluxus journal, Fluxus annuals and (in the form of boxes) anthologies with contributions from various artists. When Maciunas started work for the US Army in the autumn of 1962 in Wiesbaden, where he organised the Fluxus festival of the latest music (an event retrospectively counted as the beginning of Fluxus), he saw himself as a 'trans-Atlantic communicator' of new 'concretistic' art forms.

The alien idiosyncracy of Maciunas's work as an artist was a reflection of both the aims of the Fluxus movement and the artist's own understanding of his task. The Fluxus artists were not concerned with symbolic representation, but only with defining a framework within which and against which real events could be thrown into relief. For example, a lamp would be turned on and off or attention drawn to the background hum of conversation in a public place; or a room would be messed up and then once again tidied; or, as in *Street Cleaning Event*, the street would be swept. Maciunas defined the essence of this form of art in his thoughts on 'Concretism'. In contrast to Abstraction, this points to ways of unifying form and content. The wooden casing of a piano struck with a hammer, according to Maciunas, produced something more 'concrete' than the keys touched by the fingers of a pianist. *One Year* is also to be understood as 'concrete' in this sense: it is a segment of everyday life, an accumulation of all the food packaging amassed by the artist within a single year. (MK)

Gary Kuehn (born 1939)
***Mattress Dreampiece*, 1965**

Wood, mattresses, screws, yellow paint, 120 x 124 x 65 cm
Acquired in 1999 through the Museumsinitiative e.V.

The pale blue striped mattress has been folded twice, before six screws have been attached to hold it in its place in a niche in a yellow wooden block. It all seems straightforward enough, yet through this arrangement the American artist Gary Kuehn is able to draw attention to a number of the themes that preoccupied him during the 1960s. To begin with, the contrast of material qualities; next, the pressure under which material can be placed; and, finally, the comparison of volumes.

Through the conjunction of the mattress and the block of wood we encounter the contrast of soft and hard; in other works, where Kuehn used straw or brushwood, he generated the opposition of geometric and biomorphic forms. Through the addition of screws, the mattress is held in a shape into which it could otherwise hardly be brought. Kuehn treated this theme in a long series of works: soft, mattress-like materials were deformed under pressure by means of cords or rods, or they altered shape purely as a result of their own mass and the impact of gravity, or they were compressed and then held in a state of tension. In such works the artist was concerned with the 'vulnerability of structure'. Kuehn pursued his third preoccupation – the comparison of volumes – by placing objects firstly in similar, then in different relationships to each other. In the case of *Mattress Dreampiece*, we are confronted with the volume of the mattress, on the one hand in comparison with the niche cut into the wooden block and, on the other, in relation to the block of wood as a whole.

In as far as Gary Kuehn's work restrains its potential for expression to a few formal categories, it evinces a proximity to Minimalism. Yet it also goes beyond this. Kuehn seeks, through his art, to make visible the laws that govern our perceptual relationship to our environment, for example the implications of relative physical strength or the significance for us of our attentiveness in perceiving and assessing our immediate surroundings. Here, although the mattress takes up much less space than the wooden block, this material under pressure demands far more of our attention than the rest of this piece. Gary Kuehn sees the meaning of art to lie in its reciprocal relationship to life: 'Art makes life intelligible – but it is living that makes art comprehensible.' (MK)

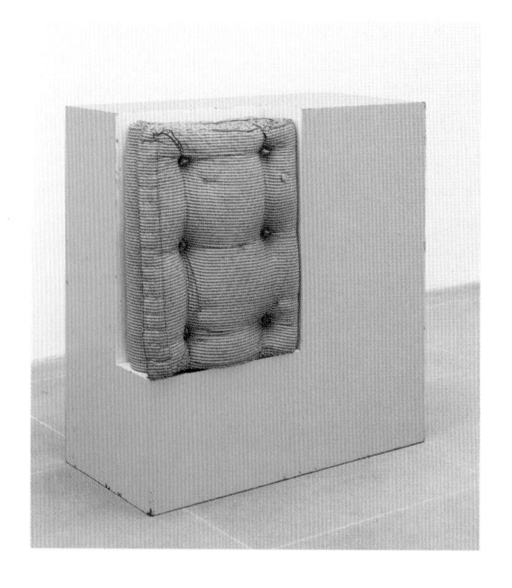

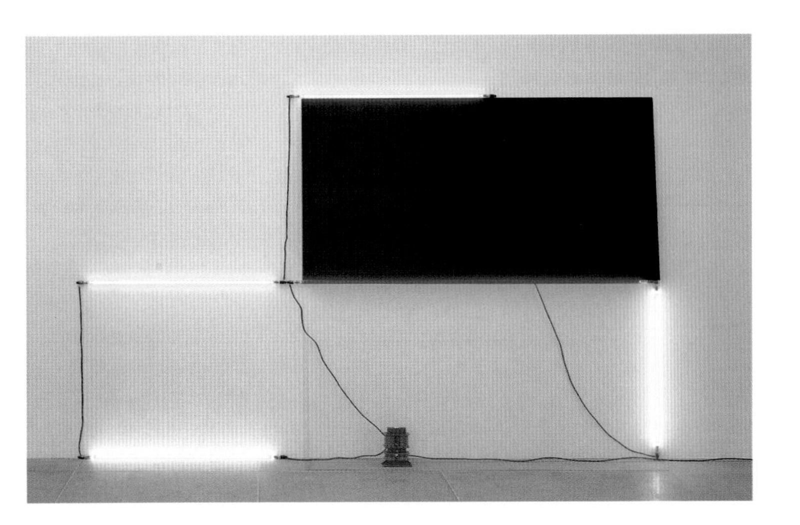

Keith Sonnier (born 1941)
***BA–O–BA, Krefeld III*, 1977 / 79**

Flat varnish on glass, red, yellow and blue neon and argon tubes, transformer, 202 x 325 x 26 cm
On loan from the City of Nuremberg (where acquired in 1990 with funds from Faber-Castell)

'*Ba-o-ba* is a demotic Franco-Haitian term meaning a bath / shower of colour or light. It describes the effect of light on the skin and the body — much as the sensation of moonlight might be expressed — as a physical, suggestive power of attraction that emanates from a natural or an artificial source. The *BA–O–BA* series was started in 1969, in order to render perceptible experiences of seeing and physical phenomena in A SINGLE visible form.' This was the explanation offered by Keith Sonnier in 1979, when he resolved to execute three works derived from a larger series of sketches for the *BA–O–BA* series for his exhibition at the Museum Haus Langen in Krefeld. The work illustrated here was one of this three. Frequently projects were first realized years after being devised.

This neon sculpture consists of a glass panel (leaning against the wall and half covered with black varnish) and coloured neon tubes. These last are either horizontally or vertically attached to the glass panel or the wall. Unlike fluorescent lighting, neon is not produced in a standardized form but can be manufactured according to requirements in a wide variety of shapes and colours. It has been very variously used in advertising, and it has been a material favoured by artists since the 1960s. While Bruce Nauman, for example, has been concerned in his own work with the inversion of script (prompted by the experience of neon lettering in shop windows), the focus of Keith Sonnier's interest is the alteration of light in interaction with different, transparent materials. He combines thin gauzes, transparent or opaque glass or one light with another, observing the various results. In the case of *BA–O–BA, Krefeld III* the observable alterations are those of the quality of the light in the case of the three primary colours red, yellow and blue. These are mediated through their combination with black and white, through the luminosity and obscurity of the space itself, and also through reflections. (MK)

Reiner Ruthenbeck (born 1937)
***Heap of Black Paper*, 1970**

600 sheets of paper, each 50 x 50 cm, dia. (at base) 250 cm; private collection

This object is lapidary in appearance: crumpled black paper piled up into a heap to form a cone. The material is neither unusual in itself nor the construction of the piece at all complicated. Nor is there anything very special about the means employed by the artist. The significance of this piece lies, rather, in a new process: that of allowing the work to come into existence largely through the application of a basic concept. The sculptures of Reiner Ruthenbeck give visible form to elementary principles. As was often the case with Joseph Beuys, his pupil Ruthenbeck here relies on the expressive capacity of the material itself. His works tend to appear accessible because they require no prior (or special) knowledge. The concept is simultaneously simple and complex. The work of art, as such, derives from a relationship of dependence, the coincidence of specific conditions and the situation that results. In this heap of crumpled paper (which exists in both black and white versions), 600 square sheets have been crumpled, one after the other, and each allowed to fall on exactly the same spot. The principle and the law of gravity are evident in the result. They can be found in the even distribution of the crumpled paper and in the almost exact circle that has been formed out of this ostensible chaos. As a silhouette, the heap of paper is triangular. While neatly stacked, the paper would have formed a cube that would have been heavy. It has now radically altered its shape along with its volume, and also thereby its apparent weight. Here we find a demonstration of Ruthenbeck's interest in a 'return to elementary principles' and a reunion of opposites. (MK)

Richard Long (born 1945)
***Malberg Circle*, 1990**

142 blocks of sandstone,
dia. (floor area) 400 cm
On loan from the City of Nuremberg
(where acquired in 1991)

According to the instructions for displaying the 142 sandstone blocks, no single one may touch another, each is to stand as upright as possible and be evenly distributed with regard to size and height. The reddish sandstone comes from Malberg, on the fringes of the Eifel. But this material is also characteristic of the architecture of Nuremberg, and Long devised the work specifically for this city. *Malberg Circle* is, therefore, not just a fundamental, conceptual principle but is closely linked to the place it is exhibited.

Long, based in his native Bristol, evolved his working methods in the 1960s in connection with his direct physical engagement with landscape. In the case of one early work he left a line in grass created by walking back and forth. He made his first stone circle in 1972. Although the works constructed in the landscape, and remaining there, are gradually reabsorbed into it, those created in an interior tend to endure. Here too the basic forms employed are the straight line and the circle, and often the title indicates the origin of the material used. Either it comes from an area through which Long has recently walked or from a stone quarry, from mountains or from the banks of a river near to the exhibition site. The material used in any given work is always of one sort only, and is arranged in accordance with strict rules. Long perceives a general significance in his work: 'My art takes materials, ideas, movement and time as themes, as well as the beauty of things, thoughts, places and actions.' (MK)

Stephan Kern (born 1955)
***Untitled*, 1991**

19 parts, iron, cast, forged and partially painted, dimensions variable
On loan from the City of Nuremberg (where acquired in 1994)

This multi-part sculpture in iron is characteristic of Stephan Kern's work and working methods. The Munich sculptor creates individual metallic forms, which he then arranges into largely horizontal floor installations. At first sight, the individual elements look like 'found objects' from the industrial domain. On closer inspection, however, it becomes clear that they are freely invented and that they only indirectly derive from those of mechanically produced rods, tubes, angle bars, girders and so on. With the help of a variety of technical processes such as modelling, casting, moulding, welding and forging, Stephan Kern produces metal collars, rods, polygonal forms, open structures and fragmented parts that testify to the manual element in their production. Stephan Kern brings a playful approach to volume and weight. That which is heavy has the appearance of lightness, and vice versa; graceful forms look powerful and vice versa. A further distinguishing characteristic of Kern's sculptures is their site-specific quality. The arrangement of the individual elements in any given piece always depends on the nature of the intended setting, and it alters as this does. The sculpture relates in the first instance to a certain stretch of floor, but also to walls, as vertical planes, and to architectural details. While, in the case of the early works, the individual parts were distributed evenly across the floor, Stephan Kern soon applied his attention to the systematic arrangement of parts into groups, with the result that particular motifs or associations of motifs would recur in a variety of works. (BS)

Raffael Rheinsberg (born 1943)
***Dead Neon*, 1991/93**

Neon tubes, floor area c 720 x 360 cm
On loan from the City of Nuremberg
(where acquired in 1995)

The Berlin-based artist Raffael Rheinsberg is the most important representative of a German art movement of the 1970s known as *Spurensicherung* [Preservation of Evidence]. Rheinsberg amasses and sorts objects of everyday use that also constitute a historical testimony and are relics of human existence. He restores forgotten facts and recalls historical procedures to conscious awareness in as far as he does not alter the pieces he finds but merely places them in a different context. Through ordering his collection in the form of an archive and displaying it in a corresponding fashion — in neat, even rows — he sharpens our response to its components. In *Dead Neon* he works with remnants of discarded neon lettering from shops in the Prenzlauer Berg district of former East Berlin, which went bankrupt after the fall of the Wall. Lettering that formerly served as advertising no longer plays this role; now it announces only the eclipse of the former East German economy. On account of their sculptural presentation, arranged in rows on a precisely demarcated area of the floor, they take on a newly aesthetic power of expression. Removed from their original sheet metal frames, broken up into separate elements, and propped up on their electrical bases, they evolve a life and individuality of their own, although they can no longer be read as words, or even as letters. Rheinsberg: 'The original reality has totally disappeared. But the object itself has more to say. One is conscious that the individual letters once formed a sign, but now it has the character of a hieroglyph.' (BS)

Hubert Kiecol (born 1950)
***Five Houses with Steps*, 1984**

Cast concrete, 26 x 48 x 31 cm
Acquired in 1989 through the Museumsinitiative e.V.

Hubert Kiecol's small-format cast concrete sculptures assume the character of archtypes of architectonic forms. His formal repertoire is epitomized by steps and houses with pointed roofs, the so-called 'standard houses'. Reduced to their essential characteristics, they are not equivalent to miniature models of habitable architecture; rather, they are sculpturally clear, thoroughly finished volumes. The compactness of the pieces is further underlined by the massiveness and density of the material concrete. Although, as in the case of *Five Houses with Steps*, a sculpture by Kiecol can also be constructed out of several equal components, we are not primarily aware of the repetition but rather the autonomy of the individual parts. Five separate houses are arranged on two sides of a right angle and, in connection with the set of steps lying opposite, they indicate a square. Yet the steps ascend into emptiness, and the relative dimensions are not altogether correct. Rising directly from the floor, without any base, Hubert Kiecol's sculptures exude a concentrated sense of calm. Their charisma and power derives from their silent presence. Statically, they exude a sense of untouchability. In his work of the 1990s, Hubert Kiecol has explored the elemental weight of brick architecture. His architectonic forms that stand on slender pillars. He has created massive blocks, stelae, benches, cupboards and monumental gates. Unlike the small-format works, which had to hold their own within a large surrounding space, these much more powerful volumes almost assail the approaching spectator. (BS)

Stephan Balkenhol (born 1957)
Man with Black Trousers and Pale Blue Shirt, 1990

Painted poplar, 246 x 48 x 30 cm
Gift of 1991 from the Lions Club Nuremberg to the Museumsinitiative e.V.

Stephan Balkenhol is a sculptor in the classical sense. He works above all with wood, yet his method of working has nothing in common with the traditional aesthetic of wood-carving. His free-standing sculptures and his reliefs, hewn from raw stumps, beams or blocks, clearly bear the traces of the manual work involved in their production. Their surfaces are raw, rough and cracked, like those of the material itself. Balkenhol heightens the sculpturally expressive aspect of his work in partially painting his sculptural pieces, for the colour is not applied in a painterly illusionistic fashion, but remains entirely subservient to the requirements of the work as sculpture. The figures are at their most truly 'alive' in their unpainted heads and hands, the natural colour of the wood recalling that of human skin. Stephan Balkenhol does not create concrete portraits or types but, rather, figures without individual qualities. He omits everything that outwardly distinguishes one person from another – deportment, body shape, facial expression, clothing, hairstyle. His figures appear indifferent: they tell no stories, represent no ideology. Rather, they offer a tabula rasa for the spectator's own imagination, emotional reactions and thoughts. The *Man with Black Trousers and Pale Blue Shirt* offers an exemplary case of this process. On a slender pedestal a male figure stands relaxed and calm, prosaically dressed in shirt and trousers. Gazing into an indeterminate distance, he offers no scope for direct dialogue with the spectator. Both keep their distance. Balkenhol's figure in fact conveys a quality that the artist has always admired in Egyptian sculptures: '... their aura of eternity and calm composure. They appear to combine the two: they radiate a feeling of transcendence but also have a real presence.' Influenced by the formal rigour of the work of his former teacher, Ulrich Rückriem, as also by the Minimalism and the Conceptual Art that flourished during the 1980s, when he was a student, Stephan Balkenhol reinvents the tradition of sculpture in as far as he redefines the theme of the free-standing figure. While his figures are placed in high positions on similarly worked pedestals, they undergo no excessive elevation as a result. Made from ephemeral materials, and usually small in scale, with restrained poses and laconic gestures, they achieve their effect entirely through the intensity of their presence. (BS)

Werner Knaupp (born 1936)
***Stations of the Cross*, 1977–79**

14 sheets, charcoal on paper,
each sheet 105 x 75 cm
On loan from the City of Nuremberg
(where acquired in 1988)

The collection embraces work from several distinct phases of Werner Knaupp's career. In the early ballpoint pen drawings, made in the 1960s, he mainly transformed landscape motifs into a series of flat, stylized forms, as in the case of *Lofoten*. In the early 1970s Knaupp abandoned this approach in favour of a radical new beginning as a figure draughtsman. Knaupp's *Stations of the Cross* consists of a group of fourteen charcoal drawings, in which the artist responds to his encounters with illness and mortality. Twelve of the drawings were made in 1977/78 in response to the experience of working in a psychiatric hospital in Bayreuth. Two further sheets belong to a group of ripped heads that Knaupp drew after a period of working in Mother Theresa's hospice in Calcutta. Except for the rendering of the Crucifixion, the drawings do not reflect the traditional iconography of the Bible; rather, they show a human Way of the Cross. Sorrow, pain, illness, decay and death are presented without any sentimentality and with an urgency that testifies to personal experience. The intensity of Knaupp's engagement with subject or motif is characteristic. Repeatedly, he exposes himself to extreme situations – for example, long sojourns in the mountains or journeys through the desert. These fundamental experiences become a crucial point of reference in his work.

(BS)

Horst Antes (born 1936)
***Figure (Woman World)*, 1959 / 60**

Egg and oil distemper on grey cotton cloth, 119 x 69.5 cm
Gift of Marianne and Hansfried Defet

Horst Antes was one of the first artists in Germany to leave Abstract Expressionism behind in the late 1950s. Influenced by HAP Grieshaber, his teacher at Karlsruhe, and an interest in the work of the artists of the COBRA group (above all Asger Jorn) and of Willem de Kooning, he evolved a richly coloured New Figuration. In his early work red was the dominant chromatic element. The pictures seem about to burst out of their frames. In the case of *Figure (Woman World)* the massive torso and the arm held above the head create the impression of motifs wedged into the extreme upright format. Here we find a figure that is not merely emerging from the private sphere into the wider world (as implied in the picture's title), but that appears to be battling its way out. While in early pictures the element of colour was still dominant, from the early 1960s the figurative element came to the fore. Mollusc-like forms evolved into gnomes, reduced to heads and limbs. In the 1970s Antes painted his awkward figures deprived of torsos — the *Head-footers*. In the early 1980s, provoked by the shock of the war in the Falklands, Antes painted houses rendered in dark grey tones, with pointed gables and blue roofs, which seemed to rebuff the spectator's interest. His most recent work includes the *Date Paintings*, in which each numeral in turn is over-painted by another in order to symbolize transience and the passage of time. (BS)

Armando (born 1929)
***Head 10–7–90*, 1990**

Oil on canvas, 198 x 250 cm
Gift from the artist, 1997

The Dutch artist known only by his pseudonym Armando first came to public attention in the 1950s as a member of the 'Nederlandse Informele Groep'. His work was characterized by black and red paintings in the style of Informal Art but with decisively non-Informal titles such as *Peinture criminelle*. In 1961, with others such as Jan Schoonhoven (see p. 29), Armando was among the founders of the Dutch artists' group 'Nul', which had much in common intellectually with the German group 'Zero'. From the mid-1960s until the early 1970s Armando worked as a journalist, and he is still known not only as an artist but also as a writer, an actor and a musician. Armando occupies a unique position as a painter whose formal language has clearly evolved out of Informal Art and who regards every other sort of painting as mere 'illustration', but who nonetheless repeatedly returns to a particular historical and political theme: the morally incomprehensible contradiction in the coexistence of 'fine art' and an 'evil world', the fact that beauty is indifferent to morality. Central to his work is an engagement with the experiences and the results of the Second World War, a period that to this day weighs exceptionally heavily on relations between the Netherlands and Germany. On one hand, Armando's paintings and sculptures address themes that have a connection with the experience of war, as in the case of *Field of Combat*, *Banner*, or *Guilty Landscape*; on the other hand, he treats motifs that are effectively archaic, such as *Head* or *Figure*. These motifs are always allowed to emerge gradually from canvases painted in a very pastose, almost 'corporeal' manner.

The *Neues Museum* currently holds three paintings by Armando: *Head 10–7–90* illustrated here, *Guilty Landscape 18–11–87* and *Figure 23–7–88*, and a sculpture in bronze, *The Black Crucible*, of 1991. (LG)

Georg Baselitz (born 1938)
***The Friend*, 1988**

Oil on canvas, 250 x 200 cm
On loan from the City of Nuremberg
(where acquired in 1989)

Georg Baselitz is a painter who has never been able to see the point of non-objective painting. Since his student days he has always adopted a position clearly in opposition to the Informal Art of the generation of his teachers. He is also, however, a painter who has not only been concerned with motifs, but also with the autonomous qualities of painting beyond its thematic connection. He overcame this conflict with the help of a process that itself has a long story behind it in painters' studios across the centuries. Even the Old Masters used to place their paintings upside down in order to scrutinize the composition, because in this situation their judgement was not influenced by thematic considerations but could respond purely to formal qualities. Although in every respect a modern painter, in 1969 Baselitz identified in this element of studio practice a principle that he has since followed in his own work: he paints his figurative subjects upside down. The figurative element is not altogether suppressed, but it merges rather more with the background than would otherwise be the case.
Baselitz describes painting as a process that is necessarily just as destructive as it is creative. A new painting arises out of the destruction and overcoming of older, preconceived works. Only through the destruction of the spontaneously adopted image can the actual image come into being, and this process occurs in the act of painting. (LG)

A. R. Penck (born 1939)
***Standart-West III*, 1983**

Emulsion paint on canvas,
285.5 x 280 cm
On loan from the City of Nuremberg
(where acquired in 1988)

A. R. Penck is a pseudonym adopted in 1968 by Ralf Winkler. It was at that date that the then Dresden-based artist, who was largely self-taught and who had evolved a modern form of 'history painting' quite out of step with the state-controlled art policies of the German Democratic Republic, first exhibited in the West. Simultaneously, Penck adopted *Standart* (an invented term, combining 'standard' and 'art'), a pictographic formal language that included the 'stickmen' that became a trademark of Penck's work. For Penck, *Standart* offered a pictorial vocabulary through which it would be possible to give visual form to social phenomena using a style informed by contemporary scientific notions, and not burdened with the stereotypes of traditional history painting or of the art of Socialist Realism. In the late 1960s, the Dresden dissident and exponent of *Standart*, was hailed as a Conceptual Artist in the West. Penck lived this artistic 'double life' until 1980, when the GDR authorities forced him to emigrate. Penck's response to this enforced move was to evolve a variant – *Standart-West*. In a small series of pictures bearing this title he announced his shift from East to West without, however, providing the spectator with any clues as to how to 'read' the *Standart* text. It is, however, apparent that this picture should be seen in both decorative and also iconographic terms. (LG)

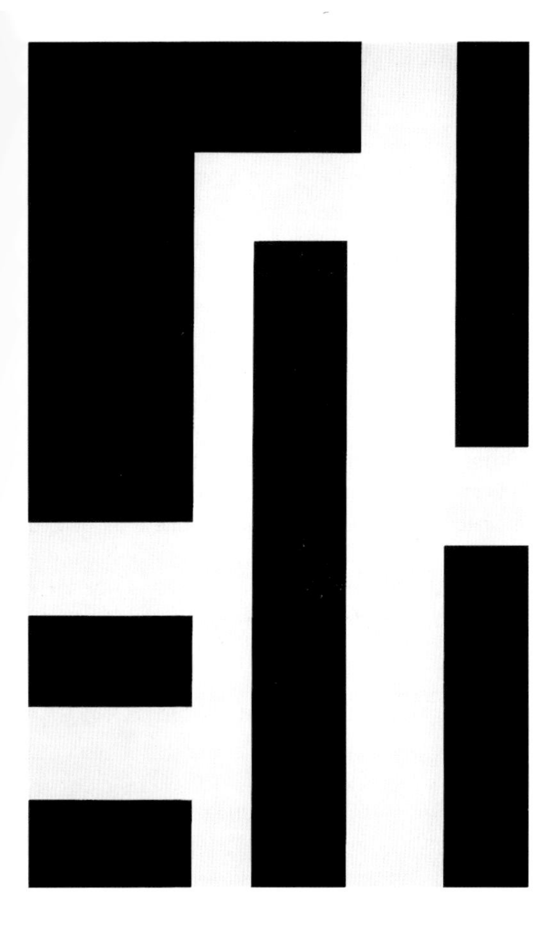

Helmut Federle (born 1944)
***Letter from a Region of my Mind II*, 1988**

Oil on canvas, 280 x 175 cm
On loan from the City of Nuremberg
(where acquired in 1989)

Constructivist art as Mondrian would have understood it and Concrete Art as practised by Max Bill or Richard Paul Lohse supply the historical background to the painting of the Swiss artist Helmut Federle. Yet this is not enough on its own to explain Federle's work of recent decades, for his geometrical compositions have evolved neither as models of a higher level of harmony, nor have they been derived from specific laws; they depend, rather, simply on positions adopted by Federle quite independently. The artist takes simple geometrical arrangements, for example the initials of his own name, HF, or widely recognizable symbols such as the swastika, and creates out of these a planar composition. This, however, is not the final goal at which he is aiming. It is, rather, a form of frame for Federle's painting which will attain its most emphatic degree of presence within it. Paint is applied, brushstroke by brushstroke, in many layers. The intensity of the painting — however chromatically reduced — fills out and eclipses the geometrical frame of the composition, and thus also banishes every element of semantic articulation that might originally have been implicit in the letters or symbols used. It is more than likely that the artist's mirrored initials will not even be noticed. Reproduction of Federle's pictures tends to render them even more puzzling than those of other artists. In fact, the subtlety and individuality of Federle's application of paint (the quality that really defines the content of the image and gives it its power) cannot be reproduced. (LG)

Sigmar Polke (born 1941)
***With Yellow Squares*, 1968**

Emusion paint on a woollen blanket,
150 x 126 cm; on loan from a private collection

Sigmar Polke has arranged yellow squares in eight rows, one above the other. Their positioning creates a criss-crossed grid structure which, although the squares are painted unevenly and positioned irregularly, permit the artist's handwriting to remain clearly recognizable. The squares are painted on a grey woollen blanket, which is already decorated with two stripes. This is an object that, above all in Germany, evokes the first decades after the Second World War. During the 1960s Polke painted many such pictures, using as a support not only woollen blankets but also fake fur, striped decorating fabric or a piece of textured lurex. In addition to Constructivist abstract forms and colour planes or lines rendered in a painterly manner, he chose subjects such as flamingos, palm trees or sunsets. Through this baffling diversity of both style and content, Polke's works do not seek to grapple with the reality of the outside world but, rather, with that of the image-world, that is to say with the norms of art; and he cites with an eloquently ironic distance the motifs he draws from this cliché-ridden realm. He is, however, above all interested in what is generally understood by the act of artistic creation and, more specifically, in the demand that artists be original. According to Polke, 'the starting point for this investigation was the sort of experience that I or any other artist might confront any day, that of sitting there, knowing full well that the whole world is expecting one to come up with something entirely new, time after time, but without any sense that something of this sort is going to emerge.' It is this expectation that Polke in fact fulfils, even though he clearly always uses the result to cast an ironic backward glance on the process. One set of clues as to what is really afoot is to be found in the way Polke's works are described by the artist. Both titles and information on the techniques employed always name the components of the picture as perceived according to the assumptions and rules of the art world. In the case of *With Yellow Squares*, Polke takes his cue from Kazimir Malevich and places on a post-war blanket the motif that is the quintessence of Abstraction in all modern art, alluding to the curious attempts of artists in the 1950s to establish their relation to Modernism through appropriating the spirit of the avant-garde. (MK)

Rosemarie Trockel (born 1953)
***Untitled*, 1986**

Wool, 220 x 150 cm, second of three versions
On loan from the City of Nuremberg
(where acquired in 1994)

This work by the Cologne-based artist Rosemarie Trockel is also made of wool. Yet, whereas Sigmar Polke uses blankets and materials that he found as the support for his paintings, Trockel's art work is knitted. Trockel started producing knitted pictures of this sort in the mid-1980s. She in fact devised designs which would then be executed by a computer-controlled knitting machine. The motifs Trockel works into her knitted images allude to a great variety of well-known trade-marks and logos, these being drawn from the worlds of business, politics and art and including the wool-mark itself, the Playboy Bunny or the Hammer and Sickle. These are usually distributed regularly across the entire picture plane, achieving the effect of an abstract pattern.

Crucial to what is probably Trockel's best-known group of works is her questioning of the clichés that allude to art itself. She asks how far can wool and knitting, achieve a recognized validity in the sphere of art, given that these are seen as 'signifiers of the female' and as 'culturally inferior materials and processes', and, as such, alien to the realm of art. Trockel poses this question through the ironic juxtaposition of domestic and craft skills with familiar, established contemporary art forms. The structure of *Untitled* of 1986, reveals how Trockel's pictures are devised with reference to the familiar. Trockel adapts the current practice of not naming works of art so that the viewer's concentration is focussed on the object itself. This particular knitted picture is arranged in horizontal colour planes in the manner of American Color Field Painting, the PostPainterly Abstraction of the 1950s. Through the use of a deep blue tone Trockel alludes in particular to the work of Ad Reinhardt. Trockel, however, counters this aspect of her work and expands on her seemingly apolitical stance through incorporating politically freighted symbols, most notably the swastika. Although this symbol is derived from an ancient Indian form, its presence in Trockel's work is certainly not without its 20th-century European significance. It is also to be understood as a provocative gesture, reacting against social norms through breaking taboos, in a way similar to many of Trockel's contemporaries. (MK)

Braco Dimitrijević (born 1948)
***Two Artists – Dialectical Chapel. Albrecht Dürer – Peter Someren*, 1989**

Bronze and marble, h 180 cm
On loan from the City of Nuremberg
(where acquired in 1992)

We immediately recognize the name Albrecht Dürer: the 'great son' of the City of Nuremberg. But who is Peter Someren? His bronze bust here is no smaller than that of the Master of Nuremberg. His name, engraved in golden lettering, is accompanied by no explanation. Is he or was he perhaps an artist like Dürer? Braco Dimitrijević, a Conceptual Artist from Sarajevo, has in fact erected this monument to a chance passer-by. There is as little to say about Peter Someren as there is about Dieter Koch, who takes the place of Someren in another version of this work. In 1976 Dimitrijević exhibited his first 'Dialectical Chapel' at the Venice Biennale: this comprised busts of Leonardo da Vinci and of another unknown passer-by. This work was accompanied by an extended caption that read as follows: 'Once upon a time, long long ago, there lived two painters, far away from any cities or villages. One day the king, who was hunting in the area, lost his dog. At last he found him again in the garden of one of the painters. He looked at the work of this painter and took him back with him to his castle. This painter's name was Leonardo da Vinci. The name of the other painter was forever lost to the memory of mankind.' Peter Someren and the other passers-by here represent the forgotten artist. The principle of coincidence here enters into a dialectical relationship with an approach to historiography in which the notion of necessity appears to prevail. Dimitrijević exploits coincidence as an 'alternative to the selective mechanisms of the power structure'. Dimitrijević aims at a new understanding of history, one that is free of the dominance of those in power. He has termed this 'Post-History'. '*The Dialectical Chapel*,' he has written, 'is a situation in which the "significant" and the "insignificant" are displayed side by side. It is a model for a post-historical society [...] When I use the term "post-historical", I have in mind a situation where it is genuinely possible for diverse qualities to co-exist.' (TH)

Joseph Kosuth (born 1945)
***Seeing Reading (To C. & A. A.),* 1981**

Green neon lettering, 11 x 530 x 5.5 cm
On loan from the City of Nuremberg
(where acquired in 1990)

'This object, sentence, and work completes itself while what is read constructs what is seen.' This sentence glows out from the wall in green neon lettering. It is a sentence that speaks about itself. It tells us that reading is an ongoing process. Only when the entire sentence has been read is it complete. And, with it, the object itself, which (as the sentence also says) is a work of art. If merely seen and not read, it remains incomplete. The work of art as such only comes into being through the act of reading. In its second half, too, the sentence speaks explicitly of this precedence of reading over seeing, for it is only that 'what is read constructs what is seen.'

The work of Josef Kosuth, an artist now based in New York, is derived from a radical analysis of the function of art. Kosuth is convinced that, since the time of Duchamp's 'readymades', art has essentially been conceptual. Art, in this interpretation, no longer deals with specific, sensually experienced qualities; it relates, rather, exclusively to ideas. It is not the object of an aesthetic and of taste; rather, it is measured by what it can contribute in the way of answers to questions as to the essence of art. In short, art has become self-referential. In this respect Kosuth quotes Ad Reinhardt's famous line: 'Art is art as art, and everything else is everything else.' Because art is its own definition, the most apposite statements that art can provide are tautologies. *Seeing Reading* is an example of this. In a related work by Kosuth, made in 1965, neon lettering spells out eight words, all of which can be related to this very line of text, its material, the language used, the colour and finally even the number of words: 'NEON ELECTRICAL LIGHT ENGLISH GLASS LETTERS WHITE EIGHT'. Through the assistance of tautology, autonomous art comes back to itself and at the same time approaches the realm of logic and mathematics. 'Yet,' according to Kosuth, 'while these other disciplines serve a practical purpose, art does not. Art in fact exists for its own sake.' (TH)

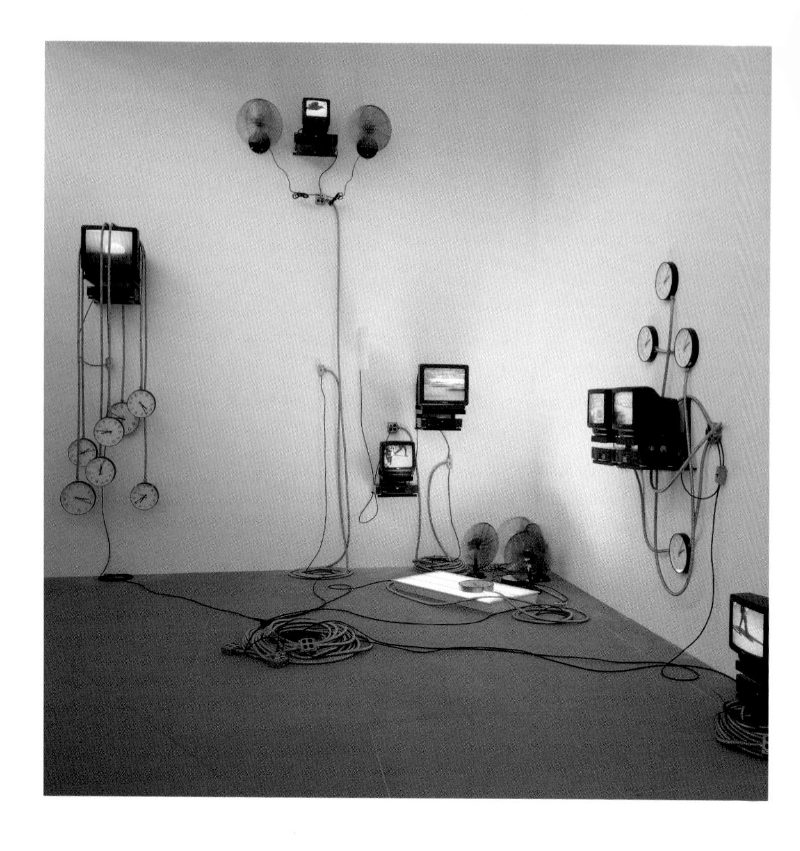

Matthew McCaslin (born 1957)
***Lifeline*, 1995**

Television set, video recorder, wall clocks, fans, ceiling spotlights, cable
Acquired in 1996 through the Museumsinitiative e.V.

Seemingly neutral, everyday objects, above all relating to the technology of television, are recurring elements in the formal vocabulary of the New York artist Matthew McCaslin. Arranged into complex room installations and plugged into a source of electricity, often all that would be needed to incapacitate them entirely is a single switch to break the current. In *Lifeline*, what at first glance appears as a chaotic and improvised tangle of wires and cables, in fact unites the individual parts into a tight, energetic system. With this networked installation, Matthew McCaslin has achieved a complex space, in which all the senses are addressed. Attached to the wall or hanging from cables, clocks measure the passing of time; rotating fans supply gusts of air; ceiling lights provide illumination. Some of the screens show traffic swishing by and pedestrians in a hurry. By contrast, two other screens show videos of birds and of a sunset, accompanied by a soundtrack of melancholy music. A flood of acoustic, visual and physical stimuli pours over the visitor who, finding himself at the centre of an energy-laden field of tension, automatically becomes the central point of a multimedia network. Even while seemingly focused on the immediacy of direct sensual experience, McCaslin also bestows visibility on the invisible: on time and energy, two truly formidable abstractions, here presented as metaphors of modern life. (BS)

Nam June Paik (born 1932)
***Enlightened Baby*, 1988**

Television and radio tubes, CD player, videos, 178 x 147 x 57 cm; on loan from the City of Nuremberg (where acquired in 1989)

The Korean artist Nam June Paik is among the pioneers of Video Art. Initially a musician, Paik became interested not only in electronic music at the beginning of the 1960s, but also in the electronic media of television and video. By altering the electrics of television sets, he found that he was able to manipulate both sound and images. In the mid 1970s he created his *Closed-Circuit Installations* as an art form in its own right (signals generated by a video-camera were converted back to images again via a monitor). Paik saw his *Multi-Monitor Installations*, created at the same time, as a new, autonomous art form, focussing on the aesthetic of television and its power to change the way one sees things and the way one behaves. Among these works, the series of video sculptures, *Family of Robot*, produced from 1986, represents a self-contained group; and it is to this group that the *Enlightened Baby* belongs. Hollowed out radios and television sets from the 1950s are composed so as to suggest a squat figure. The modern monitors inserted into the old wooden cases show fast-moving brightly coloured video-clips, supplying a flood of visual stimuli that captivate the eye. The hyperdynamism of the inner life stands in blatant opposition to the static quality of the outer form. (BS)

Christiane Möbus (born 1947)
MAN – Möbus, 1994

Shortened lorry chassis without motor, painted aluminium coachwork, 125 x 250 x 400 cm
Gift of Marianne and Hansfried Defet

The *MAN – Möbus* is a vehicle that would never have existed were it not for the imagination of the artist Christiane Möbus. With this disguised carriage she has created a sculpture dedicated, in the spirit of technology, to the time-honoured sculptural themes of power and exertion, movement and rest. Möbus, who teaches at the College of Art in Berlin, is interested in vehicles and technology. She is quite open about her preoccupation with the world of transport and feels no need to mask it within a more generalized 'critique of civilization'. She has already incorporated in her work individual vehicle parts such as motorbike petrol tanks or the rear mirrors and axles of lorries.

In making her *MAN – Möbus* she collaborated with the firm of MAN Nutzfahrzeuge AG in Salzgitter and H. Köver in Buxtehude. At first glance, this six-wheeler looks like a vehicle capable of functioning normally, yet it has no engine. Although the three axles are in fact placed unusually close to each other and there is no driver's cabin, we can discern how the vehicle would in fact move forward if it had an engine. 'The notion of power,' Möbus has said, 'lies in the three axles, which are here mounted one behind the other. The potentially very energetic object stands here in full flower, and ready to bear fruit. It is an optimum symbol of power [...].' This quality is, of course, being measured here not in terms of horsepower but in terms of aesthetic suggestion. Our experience provides us with the ability to calculate roughly how much weight the axles would be able to bear. Moreover, the chassis, with its elegant, wine-red varnished aluminium coachwork positively cries out for the load that the artist withholds. Like a beached whale, this technological colossus has been removed from its element. A vehicle deprived of both load and power strikes us as tragic. A figure of Atlas without his globe. Not unlike Konrad Klapheck in his 'machine portraits', Möbus asks machines and technology what they can tell us about humanity. (TH)

Ange Leccia (born 1952)
***Lolita*, 1988–95**

Four motorbikes and film soundtrack; Museumsinitiative e. V., acquired 1981

This group of four heavy BMW motorbikes with palmetto green metallic finish proves a little troubling. The visitor is more than likely to ask himself if he is in fact still in the art section or if he has inadvertently already moved on to design. The 'art' in Ange Leccia's *Lolita* consists in a specific arrangement of the four machines: in interplay with the work's title. Here we may presume to identify Lolita, the seductive child-woman of Vladimir Nabokov's eponymous novel, with the motorbike that appears to have been cornered by the other three. We can just make out the music issuing from its interior, from the soundtrack of Stanley Kubrick's film version of *Lolita*, made in 1962. It remains uncertain how we are to interpret the situation. Is Lolita in the process of ensnaring these admirers with her charms, or is she in fact here threatened by them? Without noticing it, we have slipped into projecting human impulses on to soulless machines, and we feel as if we are witness to a scene full of erotic tension. It was Marcel Duchamp, with his 'readymades', who was the first to make the notion of 'art', defined as such by its institutional context, into a real theme for artists. For, as Duchamp demonstrated, it was still only this context that determined whether or not an object might be seen as 'art'. The ostensible identity of the object – be it a glass-drying rack or a urinal – was in the end of no consequence. Leccia, on the other hand, selects his own 'readymades' on the basis of their narrative and metaphorical potential, and he exploits precisely these qualities in his arrangements of appliances and machines. The erotic theme of *Lolita* cannot, therefore, be separated from the erotic associations of the motorbike in its own right. This product and its styling has long been inseparable from notions of virility and potency. Leccia transposes this 'product aesthetic' into the context of theatrical installation. In doing so, he creates for the spectator as much scope for free association as for critical reflection. (TH)

Peter Angermann (born 1945)
***August #1*, 1989**

Oil on canvas, 170 x 220 cm
On loan from the City of Nuremberg
(where acquired in 1990)

Peter Angermann has been painting since the early 1970s, when he was a student of Joseph Beuys at the Academy of Art in Düsseldorf. At that time there was a great deal of serious discussion as to whether painting could still be an appropriate medium for contemporary art. One reaction to the general current of scepticism was the picture by Jörg Immendorf, *Stop Painting*. Painters were, in fact, demanding a conceptual justification for their work. In 1979 the artists' group 'Normal', founded by Angermann with Milan Kunc and Jan Knap, took as its programme the idea of normality. These artists found the themes they addressed in the world of the average consumer and of everyday life. In terms of style, too, their paintings reflected various types of popular imagery. Angermann's works often possess the character of illustrations. They resemble scenes from books for children and embrace elements taken from comic strips.

In the rural idyll of the picture of 1989, *August*, Angermann takes up a theme that has been traditional in art since the Medieval period: the depiction of the twelve months of the year. In the Middle Ages such scenes would have been supplemented with symbols and allegories of the human life cycle according to a complex iconographic programme. But they were also a starting point for the emergence of landscape painting as an autonomous genre. Angermann too takes his cue from this tradition in producing a loose sequence of landscape paintings. As a painter, Angermann sees himself assuming the 'role of a scientist' who is directly concerned with perception, and his painting reflects this concern. He has, accordingly, not painted his landscape so that it reaches to the very edge of the canvas, demonstrating by this means that it corresponds to a notion of reality, not to reality itself. The horizon, moreover, is emphatically curved; the landscape is consciously reproduced as if distorted by a camera lens. (MK)

Wim Delvoye (born 1965)
***Dutch Gas Cans*, 1987 / 88**

Enamel paint on 18 butane gas cylinders,
each 56 x 28 cm
Acquired in 1990 through the
Museumsinitiative e.V.

If there is one image that reminds us of Holland, it has to be the windmill. As souvenirs, they are embroidered on cushions or tablecloths, or painted on ceramic objects of every sort. They decorate coffee spoons or biscuit tins. In this form they are taken home, displayed there and regarded as proof of a trip abroad – originally a habit of the aristocracy to satisfy a certain representational need.

The Belgian artist Wim Delvoye takes up the idea of this commercial practice to link motifs from our cultural legacy with familiar objects of everyday use. Yet, at second glance, his works are more bizarre than they at first appear, and this is on account of his choice of supports. Exotic flowers, for example, supply the decoration for the blades of circular saws, and ironing boards are painted to look like coats of arms from the Belgian provinces. In *Dutch Gas Cans* butane gas cylinders are decorated with windmill motifs. Each of these cylinders is painted in a blue and white pattern, yet in each case in a very different style. Especially distinct from one example to another is the rendering of the windmills: by this means Delvoye alludes to the stylistic pluralism of the souvenir industry. Delvoye's work is also distinguished by a particular style of display. This is always reminiscent of the arrangement traditionally adopted in various types of collection, for example that of ornamental plates ranged on a dresser or, as in this case, of vases or milk bottles on a floor. By this means, the entire realm of the habits associated with our popular culture potentially becomes Delvoye's subject. (MK)

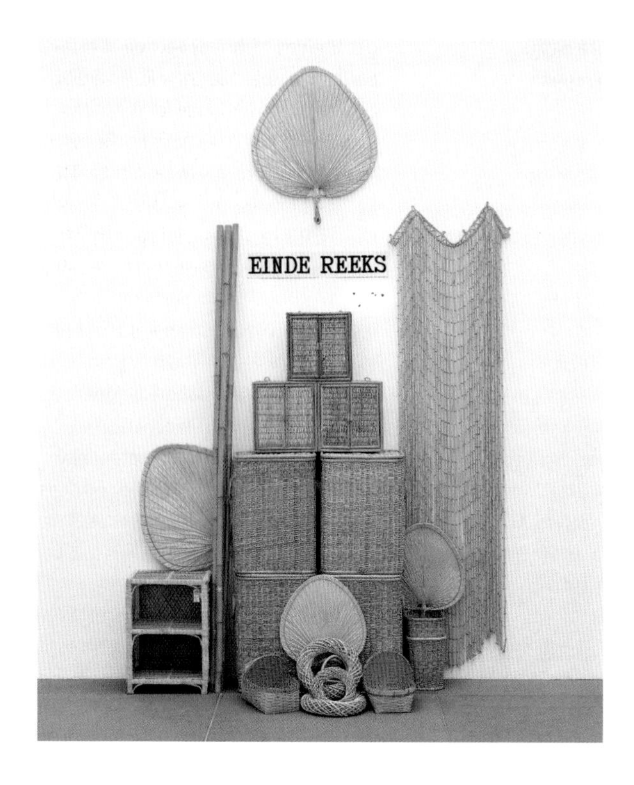

Guillaume Bijl (born 1946)
***Einde Reeks*, 1989**

Baskets, raffia, bamboo, shop sign, dimensions variable
On loan from the City of Nuremberg (where acquired in 1991)

The Dutch term *einde reeks* corresponds to the French *fin de série* or the German *Restposten* or the English *end-of-line items*: it signifies the end of a line of products that will no longer be manufactured and is therefore offered for sale, often at a reduced price. Guillaume Bijl has here used this as the title for a collection of objects made from rattan and basketry, which he has composed in a classical fashion against a wall. The objects are pushed close to one another and stacked symmetrically, the overall pattern reiterated on a smaller scale and the whole crowned with a fan.
Bijl established his reputation as an installation artist who was prepared to reconstruct entire shop interiors, and hence to introduce segments of reality within the 'non-reality' of the museum. He was himself especially concerned with the relationship between fiction and reality. Within the four groups into which the artist has nominally divided his œuvre, *Einde Reeks* does not belong among these large installations but, rather, with the *compositions trouvées* [found compositions]. These arrangements of fragments of reality are reconstructions of genuine arrangements of objects discovered by the artist. Bijl in fact regards them as sketches. 'The concept of the "compositions trouvés" alludes to the pre-existing concept of the "objet trouvé". It is always a matter of a consciously assembled recognizable composition, something that already exists in reality and that is then, as it were, found.' (MK)

Martin Honert (born 1953)
***Little Railway Box*, 1992**

Various materials, 140 x 138 cm
On loan from Helmut Schmelzer

Martin Honert, who studied under Fritz Schwegler at the Düsseldorf Academy, produces works that cannot be classified clearly either as paintings or as sculptures: they are three-dimensional pictures that take memory as their theme. Honert draws on his own youth and childhood to explore those occurrences that provoke us into spontaneous emotional reactions. Everyone is familiar with indeterminate feelings set off by images, sounds or smells. The *Little Railway Box* of 1992 is a polygonal structure with one door and ventilation slits, and it stands on a circle of grass. In its material and form it resembles the decorations of the toy section of a department store. The *Little Railway Box* appears to be an image locked in the memory, of which we have no means of telling how large it is, what function it has or even if it derives from a fairy tale or from the real world. It is an object that one might suppose to have existed in reality, and one suspects that it is just a matter of racking one's memory to discover whether or not one has encountered it somewhere before. Honert's art consists in ostensibly reconstructing what could potentially exist as a genuine memory. But he does not create his sculptural object after a real object; he in fact reverses this process. He dissects the memory, freezes the appearance of a vague notion into an image that is anchored in the present. It is the literal materialization of a mental process. (MK)

Andreas Gursky (born 1955)
***The University of Bochum*, 1988**

Cibachrome on Plexiglas, 144 x 174 cm, third of an edition of four prints
On loan from the City of Nuremberg (where acquired in 1989)

Andreas Gursky is one of those artists who, starting out in the circle of Bernd Becher at the Düsseldorf Academy of Art, have succeeded in establishing photography as an autonomous medium within the tradition of the easel painting. In contrast to the typological image series made by Bernd and Hilla Becher, the photographs produced by Gursky are each emphatically individual, and in each case the subject matter is very specific. Gursky's large-scale photographic prints possess certain recognizable stylistic and thematic constants. His subjects (usually locations in which people are to be found) are invariably photographed from a distance and from an elevated position or, as Gursky himself has said, 'from the point of view of a being from another planet'. His most frequent subjects are public places that serve as fora for human communication and social interaction.

'It's true,' says Gursky, 'that the people seen in my pictures are both characterized in relation to a specific time and possessed of a certain timeless dimension. This double connection is of particular importance in the case of *The University of Bochum*. The students lingering around on the campus are immediately recognizable as representatives of our modern leisure-oriented society through external attributes such as jeans and running shoes. On another level, however, I see them as unconscious representatives and communicators of the culture of the West – they are absorbed in their reading, and the books in their bags and hands literally contain our intellectual heritage. The duality of the new within the old is also a feature of the architecture. What we see here is ostensibly a concrete structure of the 1970s, a characteristic product of technocratic planning; yet it unintentionally bears within itself stylistic elements derived from the architecture of Mies van der Rohe and the [early 19th-century German] Classicist Schinkel.' (MK)

Thomas Ruff (born 1958)
***Block No. 9 II*, 1991**

C-print, 185 x 247 cm, third of an edition of four prints; acquired in 1999

Thomas Ruff was a student of the photographers Bernd and Hilla Becher in Düsseldorf, who came to public attention through his large-scale portrait photographs. Ruff's work clearly derives from the Bechers' systematic approach, its reliance on image series, and its restriction to a very few types of subject. He photographed fellow students, presenting their faces so that the result resembles a passport photo, with a rigidly frontal pose against a neutral white background. Despite their scale, and the extremely sharp resolution of the images, the portraits convey nothing of the personality of the recorded individual. Ruff starts from the assumption that 'photography can only reproduce the surface, not the person and his or her psyche. [...] Photography cannot penetrate even a single millimetre beneath the surface.' The identical treatment of every sitter, the same even lighting employed for every shot and the emotionless facial expressions adopted by each subject correspond to the 'angle, lighting and choice of lens' used for photographs taken for official purposes which have to be accurate images of the sitter.

Between 1987 and 1992 Ruff produced a series of photographs of buildings. Here, too, we find evidence of his rejection of techniques that would help an interpretation of the subject. Each photograph is titled merely *Building*, and the addition of a number makes clear that it is one of a series. These images contain no evidence of human habitation; the lighting is even and the view usually embracing both principal and lateral façades. As is evident in the case of *Building No. 9 II*, these subjects are in no way special: they are examples of the anonymous new architecture of the '50s and '60s: apartment buildings, schools, administrative offices, council estates, multi-storey garages, office blocks. Ruff has described these as 'average architecture, such as you might find in any German town.' 'It's the style of building that my generation grew up with, as I did, in an end-terrace house in the Black Forest.' (MK)

SCHAU,
IM AUGENBLICK
BIN ICH BLIND,
SCHAU.

Rémy Zaugg (born 1943)
***On Blindness*, 1994–97**

8 panels, gloss paint and screen print on aluminium, each 180.9 x 160.8 x 3.5 cm
Acquired in 2000

The 1960s, when the Swiss artist Rémy Zaugg was starting out as a painter in Basle, were art historically an era of Conceptualism and Analysis. Many artists no longer felt at ease with painting for its own sake and demanded a stable theoretical basis for their activity. Zaugg, accordingly, embarked on his first real debut as an artist with an intensive textual analysis of a painting by Paul Cézanne and, out of this analytical undertaking, there evolved his specific form of self-referential painting. In formal terms, Rémy Zaugg never abandoned the medium of the easel picture, which, since the end of the Middle Ages, has been regarded as the classical genre of painting. On the contrary, his work served as a confirmation of this tradition. In his own pictures, however, we do not find landscapes, still lifes or portraits; rather, we encounter texts in a rigorous typographic format in black and white, which offer analyses of every possible facet of the medium of the easel picture — its subject matter, its formal aspects, its role as understood in terms of perception.

The eight pictures of 1994–97 that constitute *On Blindness*, all executed in gloss paint on aluminium, were made for a retrospective of Zaugg's work, presented at the Nuremberg Kunsthalle in 1997. The eight images reiterate a single sentence: SCHAU, IM AUGENBLICK BIN ICH BLIND, SCHAU [Look, at the moment I'm blind, look]. These eight images are the first in a series with the same title that has since grown considerably, and they constitute the beginning of a new, colourist phase in Zaugg's work. (LG)

Roni Horn (born 1955)
***You are the Weather*, 1994/95**

100 photographs, each 26.5 x 21.4 cm,
third print of an edition of four
Acquired in 1997 through the Museums-initiative e.V. with profits from the 1996 auction of the Defet Collection and with donated purchase funds

The New York artist Roni Horn has never worked in one particular medium. To her way of thinking, moreover, the question of medium and associated method is of less importance then the posing of aesthetic questions with the help of various media. Since the 1970s Roni Horn has been known as a sculptor and a draughtswoman, but also as an artist working with photography and producing photo-based examples of the *livre-d'artiste*. Evident in her work in all these disciplines is a striving for clear form and direct impact. This appears against the background of the realization that all the forms and media of art have such a long and overwhelming history that it has now become virtually impossible to work with them in a direct and unself-conscious fashion.

Iceland has preoccupied Roni Horn for many years. For a period of several weeks, she travelled through the country accompanied by a young, blond Icelandic woman, Margrét Haraldsdottir Blöndal, and photographed her companion while swimming at the moment when her head popped up out of the water. Horn then assembled one hundred of these photographs, each with the same view, into seventeen series; together these are arranged into a continuous frieze along four walls. Horn selected only those shots in which the subject is looking directly at the lens, and hence at the spectator. Through thus limiting the potential range of images, the slightest differences between them stand out all the more clearly. (LG)

Ferdinand Porsche (1875–1951)
***Volkswagen Beetle Type 1*, 1948**
(Basic model designed 1937/38)

Metal coachwork,
h 154 cm, l 407 cm, w 154 cm
Manufacturer: Volkswagenwerk, Wolfsburg, Germany

Like almost no other object the *Beetle* is a symbol of the rebuilding of Germany after the Second World War and for the (West) German 'economic miracle'. The first designs date from the pre-war period: it was in the early 1930s that the engineer Ferdinand Porsche embarked on the construction of a *Volkswagen* [Peoples' Car], which was then put into production during the National Socialist era. Yet, with the exception of a few prototypes of the 'Strength-through-Joy Car', the Volkswagen factory established in Wolfsburg in 1938 produced vehicles largely for the German Army. Not long after the end of the war the partially destroyed factory (by then re-named British Motor Works) went into production again — one of the first in Germany to do so. In 1947 the plant had already produced 9,000 cars based on the model designed by Porsche. By 1950 100,000 *Beetles* had rolled off the assembly line, and in 1981 (by which date production had switched to Mexico) the total reached 20,000,000. The basic shape of the *Beetle* had hardly changed at all since that of the first design; individual details, by contrast (the rear window, the headlights, the rear indicator lights and so on) have altered considerably; and then there were the countless technological improvements. The coachwork itself evinces a clear tendency to streamlining. With its rounded body and its aerodynamically shaped rear mudguards, this vehicle really does resemble a stylized version of the insect that inspired its name.

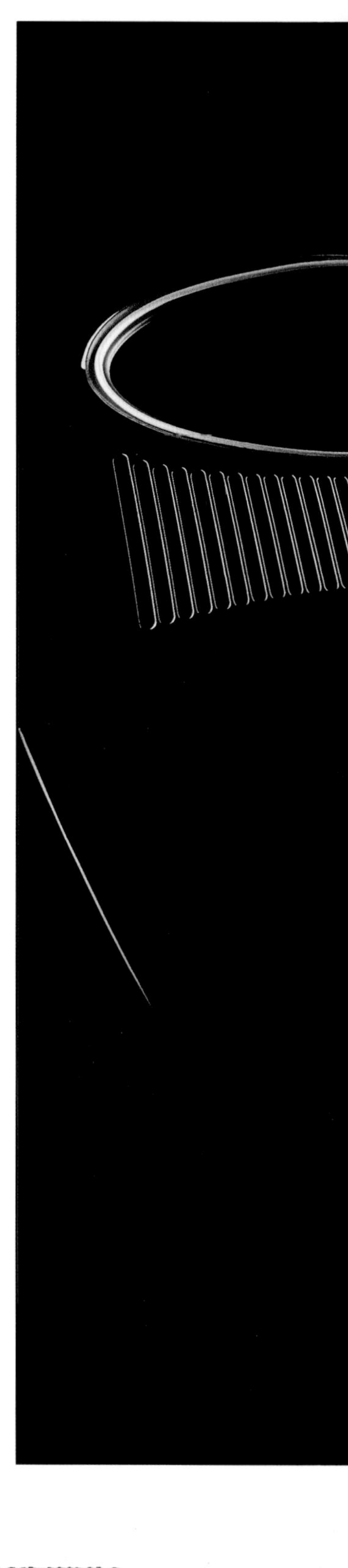

Paul Fuller
***Wurlitzer 1100* Jukebox, 1948**

Chromium-plated metal, wood with walnut veneer, acrylic glass,
h 146 cm, w 77 cm, d 65 cm
Manufacturer: The Rudolph Wurlitzer Company, North Tonawanda, NY, USA

The Golden Age of the jukebox occurred directly after the end of the Second World War. Among the best-known jukebox manufacturers was the firm founded by Rudolph Wurlitzer, who had emigrated to America from Germany. Since 1934 the Rudolph Wurlitzer Company had employed the designer Paul Fuller. Fuller's last jukebox design for the company was model number 1100, a considerable technological improvement on earlier models. Such jukeboxes are emblematic of the enormous influence of America on European popular culture in the post-war era. They brought a new sort of music to Europe , which proved a revelation, especially for the youth of post-war Germany. Along with Coca-Cola, this new music seemed to embody the essence of the 'American Way of Life'.

American melamine tableware, 1950s

Melamine in a variety of colours;
h 4 to 11 cm, dia. 15 to 30.7 cm
Manufacturer: Burroughs MFG Corp., Boonton, NY, USA; R. R. Mallory Plastics Inc., Chicago, USA

Shortly before the Second World War a new synthetic material appeared on the market: melamine. It was to establish the basis for the enormous success of plastic tableware in the post-war period. Yet again, America took the lead; there, melamine had already begun to make its presence felt in the nation's homes by the end of the 1940s. On account of its great variety in terms of colour and, above all, its resistence to chipping or cracking, plastic offered formidable competition to ceramic crockery, and the more so as it proved that established designers such as Russel Wright or George Nelson were prepared to work with it.

Coca-Cola Poster: 'Drive refreshed'

From an advertising campaign of c 1950

The encounter between Europe, and in particular Germany, with the 'Coca-Cola culture' of American soldiers during the Second World War and shortly thereafter, was very rapidly to introduce lasting changes to lifestyle. And in the realm of design the phenomenal global impact of Coca-Cola advertising proved extraordinarily influential, not only in terms of the distinctive style of the lettering and the bottle (described by the American designer Raymond Loewy as 'one of the most successful instances of product packaging in our time'), but also as an exemplar of the new marketing strategies clearly intended to reach the broad mass of the population, with texts reduced to a catchy slogan and images calculated both to communicate and to appeal.

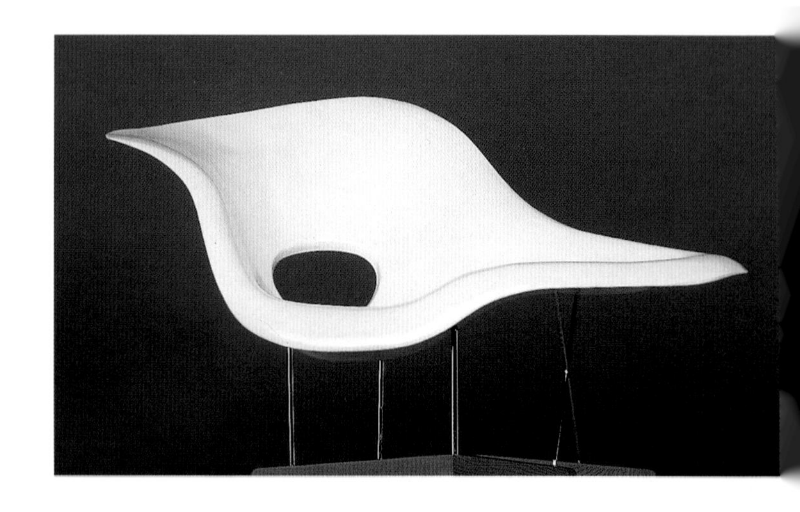

Charles and Ray Eames (1907–87 and 1912–88)
***La Chaise* armchair, 1948**

White polyester strengthened with glass fibre, rounded iron rods, varnished wood, h 88.5 cm, w 150 cm, d 80 cm
Manufacturer: Vitra AG, Basle, 1990, Switzerland

'Organic design' was the catchword for furniture designers in the 1950s. Among its most important pioneers were Charles Eames and his wife Ray, whose armchair of 1948, *La Chaise*, was made for a competition organised by the Museum of Modern Art in New York. The graceful lightness of this piece of furniture was intended to be optically accentuated through the rounded opening at the back of the moulded seat. The result was an organic form that did not conceal a certain proximity to contemporary sculpture. The name of this piece is not only the French term for 'chair', but also an allusion to the sculptor Gaston Lachaise, who was a friend of the designers.

Vladimir Kagan (born 1927)
Armchair no. 500 and stool no. 504 from the *Tri-symetric* series, 1958

Polished aluminium, red leather, respectively: h 81.5 cm, w 55 cm, and h 33 cm, w 53.5 cm, d 72 cm
Manufacturer: The Vladimir Kagan Design Group Inc., New York, NY, USA

One of the most notable American exponents of 'organic design' was an immigrant of German-Russian origin, Vladimir Kagan. His unusual furniture designs – often incorporating biomorphic supports made of cast aluminium – were rapturously received, customers and converts including large American companies such as General Electric or General Motors, but also Hollywood stars like Marilyn Monroe.

Isamu Noguchi (1904–88)
Couch Table, 1950

Black varnished walnut, glass table top, h 38 cm, w 128 cm, d 91 cm
Manufacturer: Hermann Miller Inc., Zeeland, Michigan, USA

This table, designed by the Japanese-American sculptor Isamu Noguchi, is one of the most outstanding examples of the biomorphic-organic shaping of form. In 1939 the artist had already designed a first version of this table for the then Director of the Museum of Modern Art in New York, A. Cooper Goodyear, and this was in fact his first furniture design to be executed. When, some time later, Noguchi encountered an unauthorizzed adaptation of his design, he decided to go on the offensive and to market his own version of the table.

Arne Jacobsen (1902–71)
Chair no. 3100, known as the *Ant*, 1952

Plywood (beech), chromium-plated steel tubes, h 77 cm, seat h 44 cm, w 48 cm, d 48 cm
Manufacturer: Fritz Hansen, Copenhagen, Denmark

Arne Jacobsen, widely regarded as the most important Scandinavian designer of the 20th century, had an enormous influence on furniture design in Europe in the 1950s with his organically stylized shapes. His chair number 3100, better known as the *Ant*, clearly draws on the example of the DCM designed by Charles Eames from the point of view of technology, but in other respects it goes far beyond the American design. The strength of the plywood and the use of lateral indentations — features contributing to the overall zoomorphic character of the design — are precisely attuned to achieve elasticity in the backrest; the steel tubing used for the legs (of which there were originally intended to be only three) is as thin as is physically practicable. The result is an extremely light stacking chair that brilliantly realizes the notion of truly modern furniture suited to industrial production processes. Not only was the 3100 the first Danish chair design to be mass-produced on a large scale; it was also to prove the most commercially successful piece of furniture designed by Jacobsen.

Arne Jacobsen (1902–71)
***Egg* armchair, 1957**

Polyurethane, foam-rubber stuffing covered in reddish orange fabric, steel, aluminium, h 106 cm, w 87 cm, d 78 cm
Manufacturer: Fritz Hansen, Copenhagen, Denmark

One of Jacobsen's most visually striking pieces of furniture was made in connection with the construction and decoration of the SAS Royal Hotel (for the Scandinavian Airlines System) in Copenhagen in 1956–61: this was the *Egg* – an idiosyncratic interpretation of a wing chair with integrated armrests. The unusual shape of this chair is a reflection of the 'organic design' of the 1950s, with its softly modelled seat ready to receive the sitter's body and optically separated from the base by the short central shaft on which it rests. The egg shape devised by Jacobsen for this chair was conceived for mass production in plastic. This made Jacobsen one of the first Scandinavian designers to use a material that the post-war world was just beginning to discover as potentially suitable for furniture. As it was to prove, the introduction of plastic necessitated new production methods. Extreme precision was required in shaping the mould so that the coverings, whether of leather or of textile, could be exactly matched to the contours of the underlying form.

Henning Koppel (1918–81)
Jug no. 992, 1952
Bowl no. 980, 1948

Silver 925 / 1000, chased, and mounted, respectively h 29 cm, l 22 cm, w 15 cm, and h 16 cm, w 40 cm, d 38.5 cm
Commissioned by Georg Jensen Silberschmiede, Copenhagen, Denmark
Long-term loan from the Benno and Therese Danner'sche Kunstgewerbestiftung, Munich

In 1951 Hennig Koppel won the gold medal at the IX Triennial Competition in Milan for his extraordinary bowl number 980. Like the jug designed a few years later, this has been recognized as among the outstanding achievements of modern work in silver both on account of its form and the quality of its workmanship. The jug and bowl show especially clearly how Koppel translated everyday utensils into abstract-sculptural objects, the aesthetic value of which derives from the interplay between rounded body and curved lines and the reflecting light of the undecorated smooth surfaces.

Timo Sarpaneva (born 1926)
***Hiiden Nyrkii* ('Devil's Fist') vase, 1950 / 51**

Sandblasted and etched colourless glass, h 29.5 cm, w 12 cm, d 11 cm
Manufacturer: Iittala, Ahlström, Finland

Timo Sarpaneva produced the first of several remarkable series of glass objects for Iittala in 1950. Prominent among these was the vase *Hiiden Nyrkii* ['Devil's Fist'] — a sculptural object of asymmetrical biomorphic character that clearly reflects the character of contemporary sculpture, for example the work of Henry Moore or Barbara Hepworth.

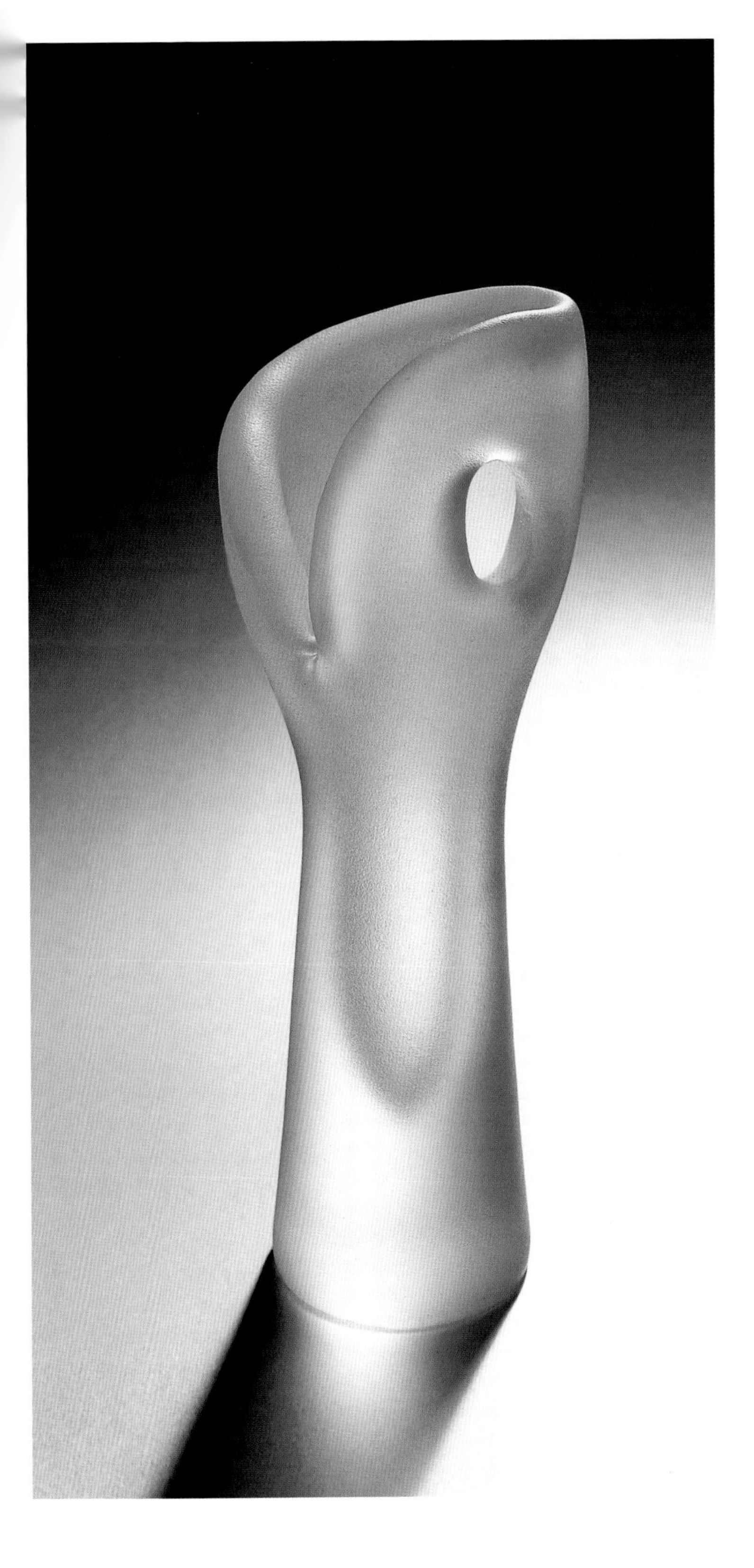

Philippe Charbonneaux (born 1917)
***Téléavia* television set, model P 111, c 1957**

Metal, varnished in brown and ivory, brown-varnished wood, h 140 cm, w 60 cm, d 73 cm
Manufacturer: Téléavia, France

In the decades following the end of the Second World War television spread with astounding rapidity. In France, for example, the number of sets owned by 1953, 60,000, had risen by the end of the decade to 1,300,000. A similar increase occurred in Great Britain, Italy and West Germany. In line with this development, the number of designers working with this novel product also gradually increased. The uninspired wooden 'boxes' of the earlier years of television now gave way to the first designs truly determined by the nature of the apparatus. Among the most unusual designs of this period was the television manufactured by Téléavia, its controls supported on x-shaped legs running on casters. To this lower section, which drew its inspiration from furniture design, was attached the swivel-mounted picture tube, its own design derived from the principles of streamling. In this combination, Philippe Charbonneaux, a designer working primarily with cars, hit upon a striking solution for a still relatively new and unfamiliar design task.

Carlo Mollino (1905–73)
Coffee table from the *Arabesco* series, c 1950

Plywood (beech), colourless glass,
h 46 cm, w c 53 cm, l 129 cm
Manufacturer: Zanotta S.p.A., Nova Milanese, Italy

The work of Carlo Mollino is an outstanding example of Italian imagination in the realm of furniture design. His first *Arabesco* table, which established the basic shape for a long series of designs, was made in 1949 for the living room of the Casa Orenga in Turin.
The idiosyncratic character of this biomorphic-organic entity is the result of the diverse character of its two principal components: the glass table top and the plywood stand. The outline of the former was derived from a drawing by Leonor Fini showing the back view of a 'reclining female form'. The undulating stand with its amoeba-like openings is in part related to motifs to be found in the paintings of the Surrealist Salvador Dalí or in the reliefs of the sculptor Hans Arp, but it also reveals the inspiration derived from aeroplane design. To achieve minimal weight in the wings, for example, ribbed surfaces could be reduced by means of holes. Mollino's abilities both as builder and as architect are also evident in the subtly static bracing of the undulating stand by means of the two glass panes. In addition to his work as an architect and furniture designer, Mollino was active as a photographer and as a fashion designer; he also built racing cars (driving these himself), designed drawing machines for the production of perspective views, drift-correction devices for aeroplanes, and chain drives for bicycles. For his work with plywood — which demonstrates both his extraordinary knowledge of materials and his genius for invention — he was granted several patents.

Wilhelm Wagenfeld (1900–90)
***Combi* combined record player and radio, 1954/55**

Olive-grey, ivory and red plastic,
h 12 cm, w 31 cm, d 29 cm
Manufacturer: Braun AG, Frankfurt am Main

While Wilhelm Wagenfeld only briefly collaborated with the manufacturers Braun, the consequences were considerable, bringing a fundamental change to the nature and appearance of the company's products. In 1954 the brothers Arthur and Erwin Braun met Wagenfeld for the first time and commissioned him to design a plastic case to contain both a radio and a record player. The result was the first appliance to embody the 'Braun Reform' that was to make its mark on German design over the following decades. This development, however, was not so much the direct result of Wagenfeld's designs (the *Combi* itself was not a commercial success, and Braun commissioned no more designs from Wagenfeld) as it was of those of Hans Gugelot and his students at the College of Design in Ulm, and above all those of Dieter Rams, the long-term chief designer at Braun. In comparison with the work of these designers, Wagenfeld's *Combi*, with its softly modelled front panel, its half-recessed red tuning and volume knobs and its trapezoidal dial was much closer to the rounded forms characteristic of the 1950s. The *Combi* was conceived for a gymnastics class devised for Braun employees by Ursula Tritschkowa: this in itself, part of a novel concept of health in the workplace, was as remarkable in its way as Wagenfeld's design.

Angelo Mangiarotti (born 1921) and Bruno Morassutti (born 1920)
***Secticon* table clocks, 1956–60**

White, red and colourless plastic, metal,
h 8.5 to 24 cm, max. w 10 to 13 cm
Manufacturer: Le Porte-Echappement Universel SA, La Chaux-de-Fonds, Switzerland

In Italy the extremely rapid technological advances in clock-making initially had no decisive impact on design. It was only in the late 1950s that a fundamental change began to occur. Table clocks in particular — by this time these were commonly mass-produced — increasingly attracted the attention of designers as an aspect of interior decoration. The *Secticon* clock, designed by Mangiarotti and Morassutti and produced in three different versions, is one of the earliest examples of this phenomenon. Among other innovative elements in this design was the unusual shape of the casing and the slope of the clock face, which was intended to make it easier to see the time at a glance. Also notable was the eradication of knobs or other such devices on the exterior (this was even so with the alarm clock, which was switched off simply by light pressure on the casing). The *Secticon* brought new inspiration and energy to clock design in Italy, as soon evinced in remarkable work by renowned designers such as Joe Colombo, Rodolfo Bonetto or Gino Valle.

Verner Panton (1926–98)

Left: ***Heart* armchair, 1960**

Partially chromium-plated metal stand, foam-rubber covered in red textile, h 89.5 cm, w 100 cm, d 72 cm

Centre: ***Cone Chair* armchair, 1958**

Partially chromium-plated metal stand, foam-rubber covered in orange textile, h 84 cm, w 58.5 cm, d 60 cm

Right: **Armchair, 1960**

Partially chromium-plated metal stand, foam-rubber covered in mauve textile, h 76 cm, w 80 cm, d 66 cm
Manufacturer: Plus-linje A/S, Copenhagen, Denmark

After studying at the Royal Danish Academy of Art, Verner Panton worked with Arne Jacobsen; in 1955 he established his own design practice. His career as an internationally active furniture designer began in 1958 when he received his first important commission – for the remodelling of the large Café Komigen [Come Back Again] in the Langesø Park on the Danish island of Fünen. As part of the interior decoration of this site, Panton designed a chair in the shape of an upended cone. This soon entered design history as the *Cone Chair* or *Ice Cream Cornet*. In order to produce this chair on a large scale, Percy von Halling-Koch founded his own firm ('Plus-linje') and collaborated with Panton until 1962. During this time they made numerous experiments with variations on the *Cone Chair*. In 1960 a heart-shaped armchair was used in the interior of the Trondheim restaurant 'Astoria'; a version of this design in wire mesh also had enormous commercial success. The square-shaped version, on the contrary, proved less popular, and relatively few of these were produced. The *Cone Chair* was something of a phenomenon in its day; it appears, moreover, to anticipate the style of the Pop Art-inspired furniture of around a decade later.

Fritz Heidenreich (shape),
Jean Cocteau (decoration)
Vase no. K 2594, 1952

Cast, high quality porcelain, decoration with offset printing in greyish brown,
h 24 cm, w 15.5 cm, d 16 cm
Manufacturer: Rosenthal-Porzellan AG, Selb

In 1950, when Philip Rosenthal Jr became Head of Advertising in the family firm, a decisive change was detectable in its attitudes and its products. In particular, the latter began to reflect the influence of 'organic design'. One of the first results of this transformation is a product of 1952: the asymmetrically bellied vase made by Fritz Heidenreich (1865–1966) with its painted decoration devised by Jean Cocteau (1889–1963).

Hans Gugelot (1920–65) and
Dieter Rams (born 1932)
***Phonospur SK 4* combined radio and record player, 1956**

Elm wood, white-lacquered metal, acrylic glass, h 29 cm, w 58 cm, d 24.4 cm
Manufacturer: Braun AG, Frankfurt am Main

This apparatus, known as 'Snow White's Coffin', is an early example of the renowned 'Braun Line' that, as the quintessence of the 'aesthetic of function', characterized German design in the second half of the 20th century. It was seen as a positively revolutionary item on account of its transparent acrylic glass lid and the location of the radio on the upper face. For the first time, there was a single, horizontal and easily accessible control panel.

Andy Warhol (1928–87)
Poster advertising the exhibition 'Andy Warhol – Whitney Museum', 1971
Design: 1966 (as Cow Wallpaper)

Screen print on thick, synthetically laminated paper (wallpaper), 116 x 75 cm

Andy Warhol, one of the leading figures in American Pop Art, radically questioned the traditional concept of art and aesthetics through the ironic stylization and serial reproduction of consumer goods and trivial objects. Trained as a graphic artist, he first worked in advertising and designed window displays. He then turned to painting. Central to his first series pictures, dating from the early 1960s, were images of consumer goods such as Campbells Canned Soup.
The reiteration of identical images, reminiscent of the conveyor belt production methods associated with the depicted objects, because a trademark of Warhol's work. In 1962 Warhol started producing screen prints, and this is the technique he used for his *Cow Wallpaper*. In 1966 he used this to decorate a room at the Leo Castelli Gallery in New York. Warhol's installation also included a second room, in which there floated helium-filled 'silver clouds'. By this means Warhol formally took leave of painting. Warhol's relation to Modernism and his questioning of the assumption that uniqueness, authenticity and originality were essential to a true work of art could hardly have been more succinctly and provocatively conveyed. In effect, Warhol made art out of his protest against art. The first version of his *Cow Wallpaper*, with a mauve cow on a yellow background, was followed in 1971 and 1976 by further versions in a variety of colour combinations.

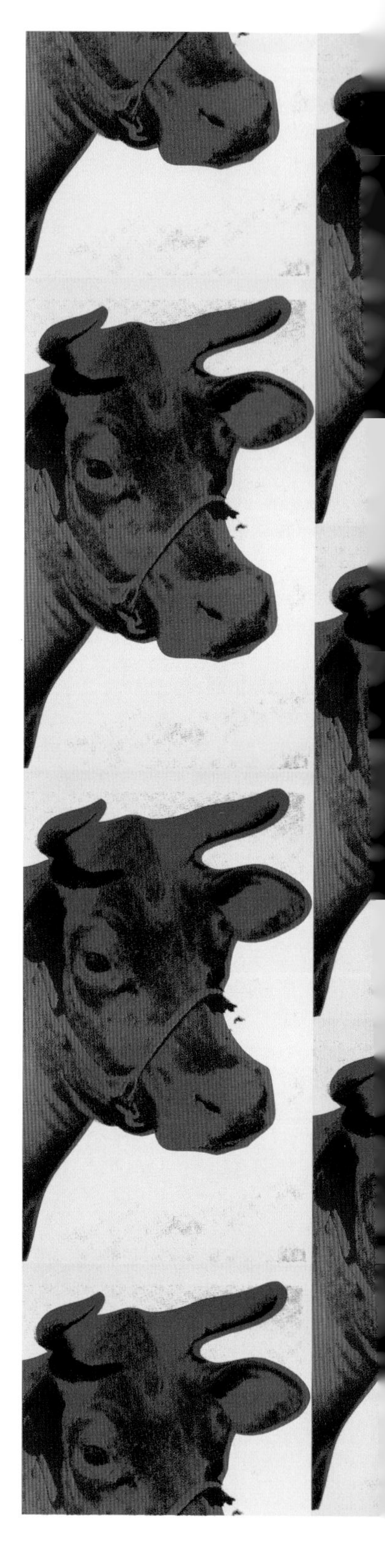

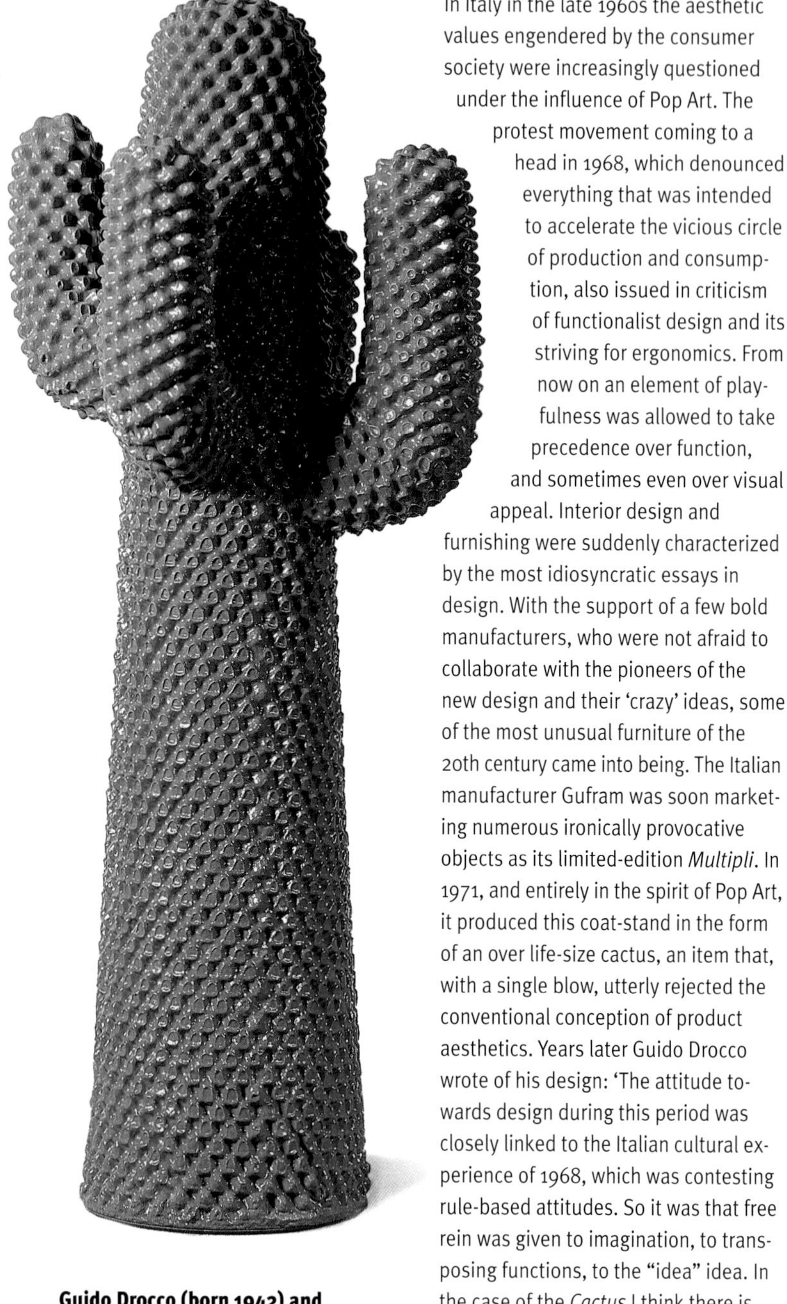

Guido Drocco (born 1942) and Franco Mello (born 1945)
***Cactus* coat-stand, 1971**

Green painted polyurethane foam-rubber, h 170 cm, w 70 cm, d 70 cm
Manufacturer (1986): Gufram s.r.l., Balangero, Italy

In Italy in the late 1960s the aesthetic values engendered by the consumer society were increasingly questioned under the influence of Pop Art. The protest movement coming to a head in 1968, which denounced everything that was intended to accelerate the vicious circle of production and consumption, also issued in criticism of functionalist design and its striving for ergonomics. From now on an element of playfulness was allowed to take precedence over function, and sometimes even over visual appeal. Interior design and furnishing were suddenly characterized by the most idiosyncratic essays in design. With the support of a few bold manufacturers, who were not afraid to collaborate with the pioneers of the new design and their 'crazy' ideas, some of the most unusual furniture of the 20th century came into being. The Italian manufacturer Gufram was soon marketing numerous ironically provocative objects as its limited-edition *Multipli*. In 1971, and entirely in the spirit of Pop Art, it produced this coat-stand in the form of an over life-size cactus, an item that, with a single blow, utterly rejected the conventional conception of product aesthetics. Years later Guido Drocco wrote of his design: 'The attitude towards design during this period was closely linked to the Italian cultural experience of 1968, which was contesting rule-based attitudes. So it was that free rein was given to imagination, to transposing functions, to the "idea" idea. In the case of the *Cactus* I think there is something else: irony. By irony I mean bracketing off and gazing unconvinced, yet amused, at what's being done and everything that arises from what's been done.'

Eero Aarnio (born 1932)
***Ball* armchair, 1963–65**

Red polyester strengthened with glass fibre, red lacquered metal, h 120 cm, w 105 cm, d 100 cm
Manufacturer: Asko Oy, Lahti, Finland

It was above all through the designs of Eero Aarnio that Finland was able, in the 1960s, to establish itself as a nation strongly associated with good modern design. Aarnio's interest in using new materials, in particular plastics, was positively revolutionary by comparison with the character of the native tradition of furniture design, which almost invariably used wood. With the help of Asko, the most innovative Finnish furniture manufacturer, Aarnio was able to realize designs that were exceptionally modern for their period. The first prototype of the spherical armchair had already been devised in 1963, and serial production started two years later. This item, often called the *Globe* or the *Ball Chair*, is one of the best-known symbols of the age of space travel, which began in 1961 when Yuri Gagarin orbited the earth and reached its first highpoint in 1969 with the first moon-landing. In numerous films and television series, this chair featured as the epitome of modernity. There was a widespread intoxication with a sense of the fantastic possibilities of the future. The supposedly worn-out path of Classical furniture design was abandoned in favour of playfully futuristic ideas, and Aarnio's armchair was seen to embody these especially well.

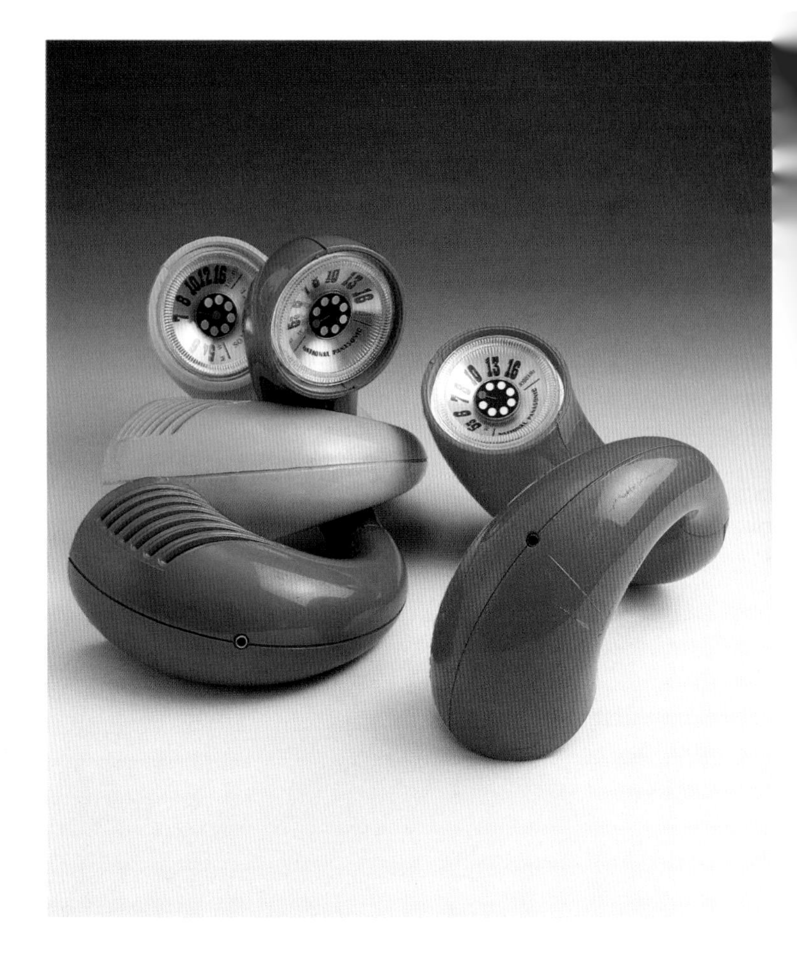

National Panasonic radio set R–72 S, c 1969

ABS-plastic in orange, blue and yellow, h 7 cm, dia. 15 cm
Manufacturer: Matsushita Electric Industrial Co. Ltd., Japan

The very rapid pace of development in the technology of radio construction from the mid-1950s – the replacement of valves by transistors, the increasing miniaturization of components – led to the transformation in the design of the casing. Equally responsible for this change was the triumphal advance of plastic during the 1960s. The injection moulding process was ideal for rounded and otherwise quirky shapes, and a wide variety of colours was now also available. While German and Italian designers such as Dieter Rams or Mario Bellini aimed above all at clarity and objectivity, around 1970 their contemporaries in Japan devised unconventional shapes inspired by the 'craziness' of Pop Art. An extreme example of this tendency is the radio with swivel-joints produced in 1969 by Matsushita. This could be 'worn' like a bracelet on the wrist and was, in effect, a predecessor of the *Walkman* first developed in Japan only a few years later.

Combined radio and cassette-recorder, model 2001, c 1970

ABS-plastic in white and black, colourless acrylic glass, h 30 cm, w 27 cm, d 27 cm
Manufacturer: Weltron, Japan

From the 1960s the commercial success of portable transistor radios was reflected in the design of other electronic appliances associated with leisure and entertainment. Soon it was possible to buy portable record players and portable televisions. Mobility was the crucial criterion and it seemed that the quest for this desirable quality would stop at nothing: even eight-track cassette-recorders like the one illustrated here were conceived as 'portables'. In Japan, as in the West, the inspiration for designs of this sort was found in popular culture and, as in this particular case, in space travel and the Science Fiction fantasies influenced by it. A recurrent form, almost a form of leitmotif, was the sphere: here it assumes more specific associations with an astronaut's helmet through details such as the lateral circular casing of the speakers or the black front panel. The model number itself relates to space travel, or at least to Stanley Kubrick's film of 1968, *2001, A Space Odyssey*. The Japanese company Weltron made other appliances in the same spirit, these including a spherical loudspeaker and a hi-fi system in the form of a UFO.

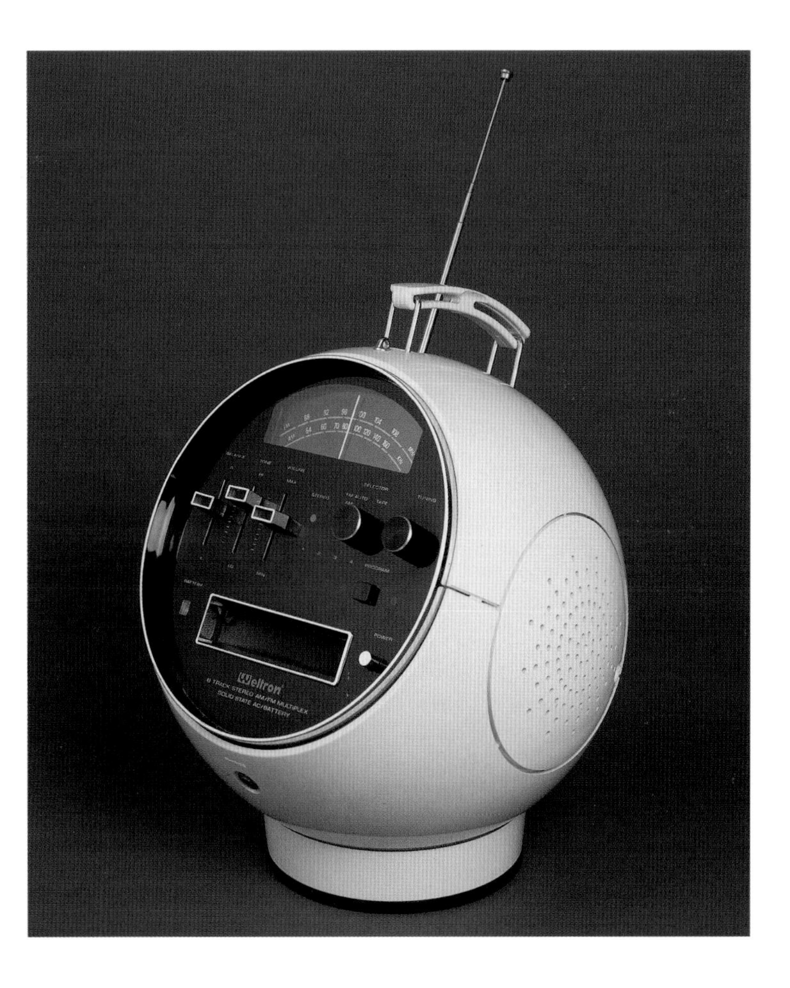

Piero Gilardi (born 1942)
***Sassi* objects for sitting, 1967**

Polyurethane foam-rubber, painted in brown, green and grey, respectively, h 45 cm, l 75 cm, w 60 cm, h 16.5 cm, l 35 cm, w 26 cm, and h 12 cm, l 19 cm, w 16 cm
Manufacturer (1986): Gufram s.r.l., Balangero, Italy

Virtually no-one looking at Piero Gilardi's *Sassi* [stones] would at once guess that they were intended as a form of seating. Both in shape and surface texture, they are deceptive imitations of their model in nature. Unlike most Gufram products – for example, the *Cactus* (p. 92) or the *Pratone* [Large Meadow] – this design by Piero Gilardi is not a stylization or an extreme enlargement of a naturally occurring form. Nothing is added and nothing is altered. Here, then, the principle of *mimesis* [mimicry], already well-established in the aesthetics of Antiquity, has been applied in the realm of design and, with it, there comes a radical break with the heretofore prevailing conception of seating. In 1968 Gilardi wrote of his aims: 'My work is a kind of tactile art. I was trying to create a fantastic nature landscape for men living among all the modern city's concrete [...]. When I was in New York, I had a 160 square-foot nature fake displayed on the floor of Fischbach's gallery. Adults walked all around it and were amused and intrigued. Then a bunch of teenagers came in and in the most casual way sat and lay down on it and continued their talking. They were absolutely right and they got the message I wanted to express.'

Studio 65
***Capitello* armchair, 1971**

White-painted polyurethane foam-rubber,
h 82 cm, w 110 cm, d 120 cm
Manufacturer (1986): Gufram s.r.l., Balangero

Studio 65 consisted of three designers: Piero Gatti (born 1940), Cesare Paolini (1937–83) and Franco Teodoro (born 1939). In the late 1960s they had produced a piece of furniture that rapidly came to be seen as an icon of Pop Art-inspired 'anti-design' — the celebrated bean-bag chair *Sacco*. With their *Capitello* armchair of 1971 they went one step further, for this piece of furniture belongs in the same context as the *Sassi* (left) also produced by Gufram. In the case of *Capitello*, however, the model was not found in nature but in the realm of architecture: it was an Ionic capital, a form associated in the first instance with the temples built in Ancient Greece. Instead of being made of hard marble, however, this armchair is made of soft foam-rubber, weatherproofed through the application of a special varnish that provides a rubber-like surface. The influence of 'Radical Design' is here unmistakeable. This movement, an offshoot of *architettura radicale* (a concept evolved by the art critic Germano Celant), started in Italy in the late 1960s at the time of a wave of student protests and a parallel tendency to radicalism in art. Its leaders were as critical of the persistence of rationalism and functionalism in Italian furniture design as they were of the consumerism and lack of aesthetic awareness that was fostered by industry. Objects such as the *Capitello* were a deliberate challenge to both.

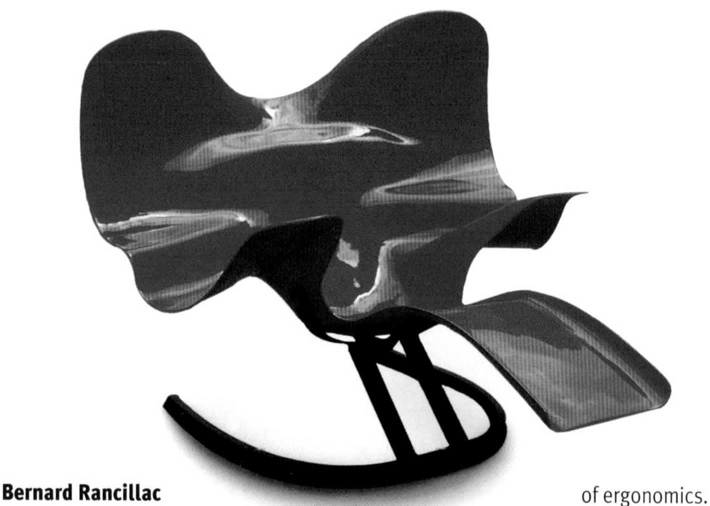

Bernard Rancillac (born 1931)
***Éléphant* armchair, 1966 / 67**

Red polyester strengthened with glass fibre, black-varnished metal, h 60 cm, w 142 cm, d 160 cm
Manufacturer: Galerie Lacloche, Paris, France

The *Éléphant* armchair was the most popular object to be devised by the French sculptor and designer Bernard Rancillac. What at first glance appears to be a most unusual shape was in fact the outcome of Rancillac's complex studies of the positions adopted by the human body at rest. The *Éléphant* armchair as a timely response to 'organic design' combined with a concern for the principles of ergonomics.

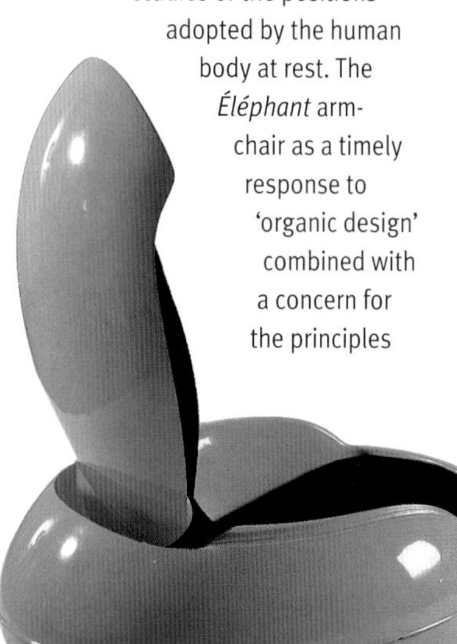

In 1985 production of the chair was resumed by the furniture manufacturer Roudillon.

Peter Ghyczy (born 1940)
***Senftenberg Egg* armchair, 1968**

Yellow-varnished polyurethane hard foam-rubber, black cushion, h 101 (seat h 45), w 75 cm, d 84 cm
Manufacturer: Reuter Produkt, (West) Germany; VEB Synthese Werk Schwarzheide, Oberlausitz, Senftenberg, (East) Germany

The chair in the form of a slightly flattened egg with a folding lid was made as a student project to design a weatherproof piece of garden furniture. Peter Ghyczy, who had studied architecture in Aachen, then sold the rights to his design to the Reuter group, which later passed these on, together with the production moulds and information on the manufacture of polyurethane hard foam-rubber, to a firm in Senftenberg in the former German Democratic Republic, VEB Synthese Werk Schwarzheide. The *Egg* was copied and manufactured there between 1972 and 1974. The fact that a design imbued with the contemporary aesthetic of the West should be manufactured in the East is evidence both of a concession to the lure of the capitalist consumer society and of an interest on the part of those in West Germany in technological processes, these being especially well developed in East Germany. Senftenberg eventually gave its name to this product. In 1998 Felix Ghyczy took over its production.

Vittorio Parigi (born 1937) and Nani Prina (born 1938)
***Oryx* desk, 1970**

Blue ABS-plastic, chromium plated steel tubing, colourless glass,
h 84 cm, w 104 cm, d 67 cm
Manufacturer: Molteni & Co., Milan, Italy

During the course of the 1960s plastic triumphed in all aspects of furniture construction. Now not only chairs and tables but also cupboards and beds, even entire moulded interiors were made from this material. It was possible to find tables of every sort: side tables, small portable café tables, tea tables, dining tables and eventually also desks. The design by Vittorio Parigi and Nani Prina is a key example of how material-specific possibilites of design can be pursued and adapted with results that are as functional as they are imaginative. Through its shape and its colouring, an item that would once have been originally a sober piece of office furniture assumes a new, playful character.

Cesare Casati, Emanuele Ponzio and Gino Marotta
***Tunnel-Diskothek* installation, Hotel Grifone, Bolzano, 1968**

Colourless, white and semi-transparent green acrylic glass, metal, cushions with textile covering in mauve and pink, seats: h 66 cm, w 46 cm, d 45 cm; table: h 59 cm, dia 70 cm; wall panel: h 140 cm, l 152 cm
Manufacturer: Guzzini et Comfort, Italy

The Tunnel discothèque was decorated in a highly futuristic style with large 'cloud curtains' made of transparent PVC film that both optically and acoustically demarcated the seating area from the dance floor. By means of these 'clouds' and the panels in imitation of green hedges and bushes – both elements designed by Gino Marotta – there arose the impression of a paradisaical landscape, its artificiality enhanced

through the colouring of the other elements of the installation. The transparent acrylic glass of the tables, armchairs and stools contained fluorescent pigments that picked up the light in each table base, which in turn changed in time with the rhythm of the music. The immediately surrounding area was thus intoxicatingly immersed in ever-changing coloured illumination. The blend of ambitious technology and imaginative design can be said to have created something approaching a 'total work of art' that reflected the cultural atmosphere of the late 1960s.

Ennio Lucini (born 1934)
***Cespuglio di Gino* table lamp, 1968**

Neon green acrylic glass, aluminium, white-varnished metal, h 32 cm, max. dia. 41 cm
Manufacturer: Guzzini Design House, Recanati, Italy

Ennio Lucini was another Italian who was moved to explore the possibilities for creating lights by using acrylic glass — a material which, although it was known before World War II, only took the world of design by storm in the 1960s. A multi-talented graphic and product designer, who from 1975 to 1980 served as Art Director of the celebrated magazine *Domus*, Lucini focused his efforts on the physical properties of segments of acrylic glass with irregularly undulating edges that would pick up pencilled rays of pale green light. From its shape and design the lamp belongs to the late '60s, together with other objects inspired by pop-culture. As the name *Cespuglio* [bush] itself indicates, it was the natural world — much as in the case of the hedges of the Tunnel discothèque by Casati, Ponzio and Marotta — that provided a model for stylization.

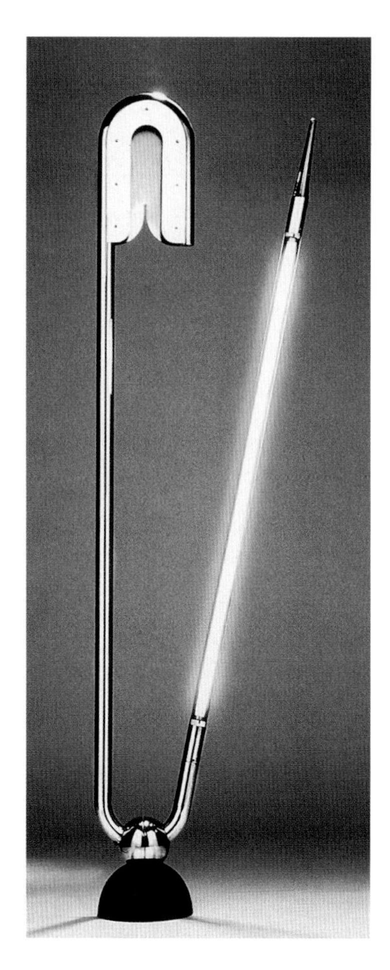

Yonel Lébovici (born 1937)
***Épingle de nourrice* (Safety Pin) light object, 1980**

Partially nickel-plated metal,
h 198 cm, w 70 cm, d c 25 cm
Manufacturer: Yonel Lébovici, Paris, France

After completing his studies in aviation technology, Yonel Lébovici started working as a sculptor and designer. He was particularly interested in light and its incorporation within sculpture. While he was initially drawn to the use of acrylic glass – a material much favoured by artists and designers in the late 1960s – he often later used metal, finding that this aged 'more beautifully'. Although Lébovici designed his first light object in 1969, his most celebrated work was produced around ten years later: this was the *Épingle de nourrice*, a lamp in the form of a safety pin. From one point of view this consists of a greatly enlarged version of a banal object from everyday life: in this respect it embodies the 'blow up' principle of Pop Art. On the other hand it is an exemplary case of the transformation of function. Here, as in other designs by Lébovici, the designer excels in his use of both enlargement and transposition.

Ingo Maurer (born 1932)
***Giant Bulb Clear* lamp, 1966**

Chromium-plated metal, crystal glass,
h 55 cm, dia. 30 cm
Manufacturer: Design M, Munich, Germany

The career of Ingo Maurer as a lighting designer got underway in 1966 with the foundation of the manufacturing firm Design M in Munich. In the same year this company produced Maurer's *Bulb*, which proved to be one of his most popular designs. The Pop Art-influenced form of an over life-size lightbulb combines elegance and simplicity with the playful lightness that was to become established as a characteristic of Maurer's work. Writing of the origin of this lamp design, he commented in 1998: 'I was, and still am, fascinated by bare lightbulbs. This started in the loo of my parents' house and has ended, for the moment, with my last work, using holography. For me, the lightbulb stands for the symbiosis of industry and poetry. I designed my first *Bulb* in a room in a cheap hotel in Venice, which is where I then had the glass for it made.' Maurer's designs of 1966, *Bulb*, *Giant Bulb Clear*, *Giant Bulb Opal* and *No Fuss*, constitute an entire family of lamps, and one that was to grow over the following years.

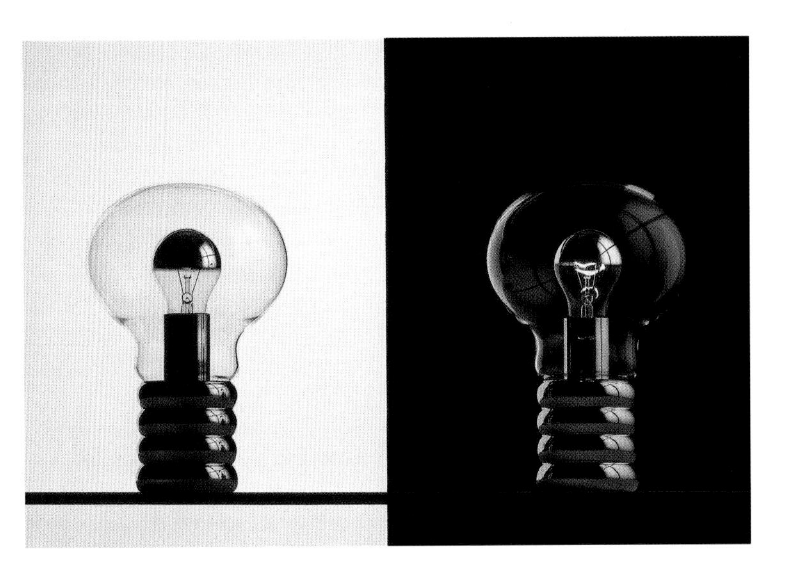

Yonel Lébovici (born 1937)
***La Prise* or *La Fiche Mâle* (Plug) light object, 1977**

Polished high-grade steel, h 36 cm, w 37 cm, l 70 cm, cable l 235 cm
Manufacturer: Yonel Lébovici, Paris, France

In the second lamp by Lébovici illustrated here the same principles are at play as are to be found in the case of the *Épingle de nourrice* (left). Yet again, the lamp has the form of a simple object of everyday use – in this case an electric plug – that is vastly exaggerated in its dimensions. On this occasion, however, Lébovici departs further from his model through the material he employs, for a plug made entirely of metal would be a logical absurdity. The conception and the limited editions of Lébovici's designs underline the close connection between art object and design object in the late '60s and the '70s.

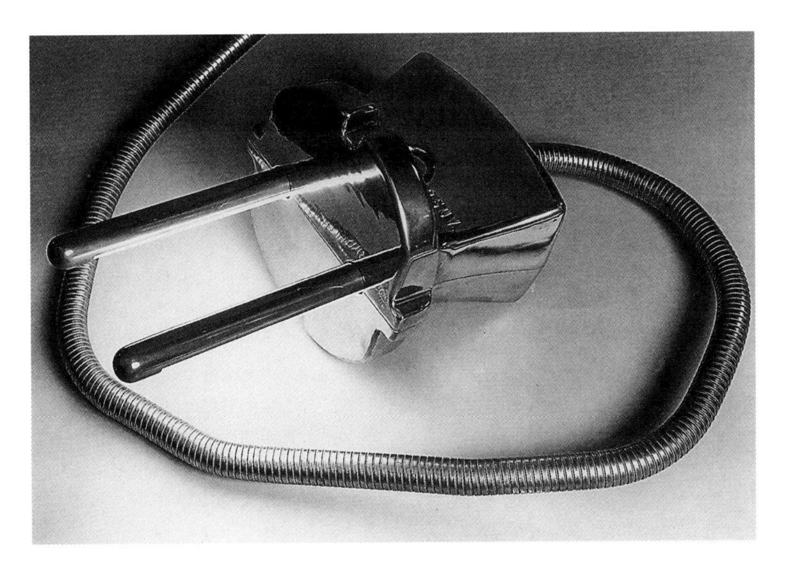

Eero Aarnio (born 1932)
Pastilli or *Gyro* armchair, 1967/68

Green polyester, strengthend with glass fibre, h 52 cm, seat h 30 cm, dia. 93 cm
Manufacturer: Asko Oy, Lahti, Finland

The production of Eero Aarnio's spherical armchair more than fulfilled the hopes of Asko that this company would attain international recognition as a manufacturer of modern furniture. As the fruitful collaboration with Aarnio continued, this reputation was strengthened. Aarnio was given every freedom to devise further similarly experimental and innovative pieces of furniture. Aarnio produced a number of striking designs, especially notable among them being the armchair called *Pastilli* or *Gyro*. This item, conceived for both indoor and outdoor use, is distinguished by its flattened spherical form, which results in an absence of stability and, in effect, offers an unusual variant on the rocking chair. However, while the traditional rocking chair is defined as such by the presence of two parallel rockers, which determine its movement, Aarnio's armchair can move from side to side in every direction. Moreover, Aarnio not only dispenses with the functional separation of stand and seat; he also facilitates an entirely different, much less fixed and rigid type of sitting posture. A report in the *Süddeutsche Zeitung* in 1968 conveys something of the first impression made by Aarnio's *Pastilli* armchair on his contemporaries: 'A Finnish furniture manufacturer with a sort of monopoly on the product, with a whole forest and its own wood workshop such as probably no other furniture concern in the world has at its disposal, astounds us with its products made of plastic and thereby demonstrates that a new material, appropriately used, may stimulate the invention of entirely new forms, as long as one does not cling to tradition. Chairs made out of two plastic moulds, shaped to form a shallow circular body with a depression to create a seat, have no longer the slightest connection with conventional chair design. And yet, sitting in these new objects is comfortable, one can rock back and forth and, without getting up, change one's position [...].' With his ideas endorsed by the great success of the *Pastilli* armchair – it is among the most frequently cited domestic objects of the late 1960s – Aarnio designed further striking pieces of furniture, for example the *Bubble* armchair of 1968 in acrylic glass or the *Tomato* armchair of 1971. A great many of his designs from this period, together with numerous later objects, are now produced by the manufacturer Adelta.

Günter Beltzig (born 1941)
***Floris* chair, 1967**

Red polyester strengthened with glass fibre, h 106 cm, w 46 cm, d 60 cm
Manufacturer: Gebrüder Beltzig, Wuppertal, Germany; (1991) Reedition Galerie Objekte, Munich, Germany

One of the most extraordinary contributions made by a German designer to the 'crazy' 1960s was the *Floris* chair, which was presented at the Cologne Furniture Fair in 1968. The anthropomorphic character of the weatherproof stacking chair derives entirely from Beltzig's preoccupation with ergonomics and function. Concerning the evolution of this design, Beltzig later wrote: 'In December 1966 I embarked on my designs for the *Floris* chair [...]. In the autumn of 1967, after the realization of three prototypes, the chair was ready. It looked like a sculpture and was the outcome of a compromise with technology, but a good compromise [...]. *Floris* was my protest against the design convention that "form follows function", and against the search for an eternally valid form. *Floris* was my "extra-institutional opposition" [...]. A concern with function determined the final shape of the chair. Those features most obviously prompted by ergonomic considerations — the precisely shaped hollow, the extended support for the thighs and the neckrest — resulted in a comfortable, relaxed seating position. The unpleasant sweating that occurs when one sits on sealed plastic moulds was prevented through incorporating air channels within these. I achieved the chair's stability without struts and without additional layers of plastic, but merely through ensuring a perfectly balanced relationship between the various planar surfaces. The result was a combination of stability and resilience.'

Ettore Sottsass (born 1917) and Perry A. King (born 1938)
***Valentine* portable typewriter, 1969**

Polyethylene, red and black ABS-plastic, rubber, h 10.5 cm, w 33 cm, d 34 cm
Manufacturer: Olivetti S.p.A., Ivrea, Italy

In contrast to its predecessors, this portable typewriter was not intended to preserve the image of the cold office machine. It suggests an altogether different image — one allied to the private sphere, to playfulness, to pleasure. The use of red bestows an emphasis on the sensual qualities of this typewriter — something that was extremely unusual for its time. Not surprisingly, the *Valentine* has since become an icon of modern design.

Ettore Sottsass (born 1917)
***Sugar* fruit bowl and *Cherries* teapot from the series *Indian Memory*, 1972**

High-grade stoneware, partially with coloured glaze, respectively, h 8.2 cm, dia. 30.5 cm, and h 27.5 cm, w 20 cm, d 11.5 cm
Manufacturer: Anthologie Quartett, Bad Essen

While designed by Sottsass in 1972, in memory of his travels in India, these items went into production only in 1987. Through the introduction of 'quotations'

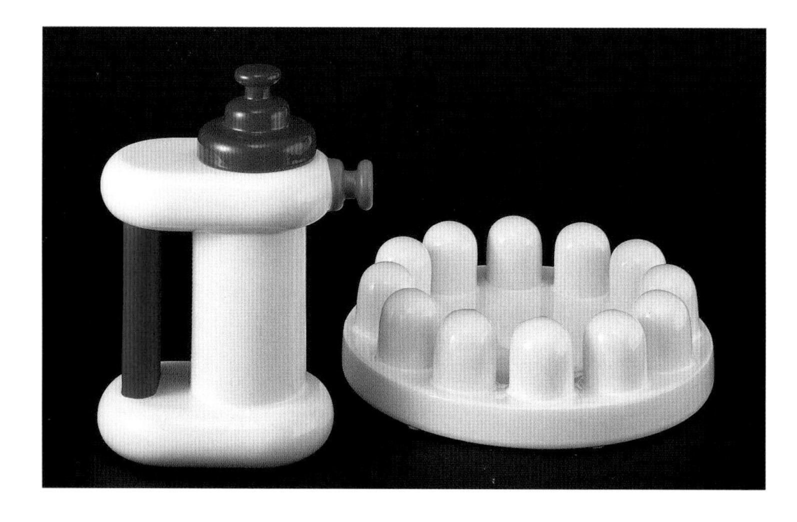

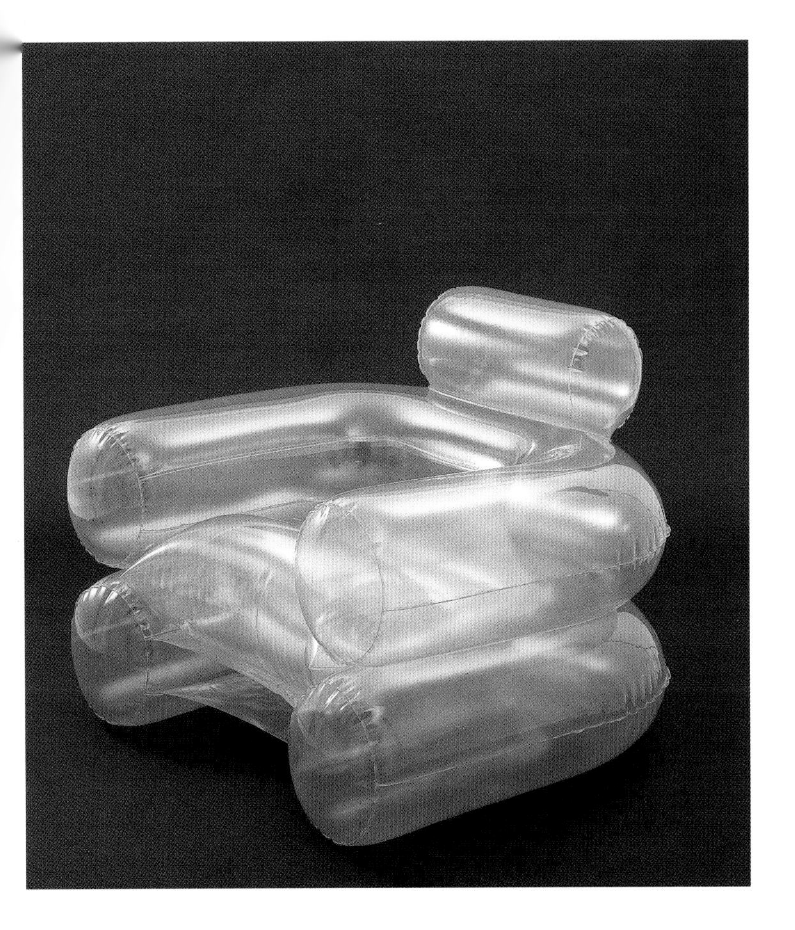

— in this case from Indian culture — Sottsass anticipates one of the fundamental design principles of Post-Modernism.

Jonathan de Pas (born 1932), Donato d'Urbino (born 1935) and Paolo Lomazzi (born 1936)
***Blow* inflatable armchair, 1967**

Transparent polyvinyl chloride (PVC)
with seams electronically welded,
h 83 cm, w 110 cm, d 80 cm
Manufacturer: Zanotta S.p.A., Nova Milanese

The *Blow* armchair was the first inflatable piece of seating furniture to be serially produced with great success. Without any additional supporting structure, the armchair retains its form and its stability entirely through its series of filled air chambers. The transparency demanded by the designers could only have been achieved with PVC film, and new production techniques (incorporating a high-frequency welding process) had to be developed to accommodate this material. With the *Blow* armchair, a light, transparent, mobile and economical piece of seating furniture conquered the living room. Implicit in this 'revolution' was a questioning of bourgeois values and traditional lifestyles, for now (the *Blow* armchair seemed to imply) neither the enduring nor the materially valuable counted for much. This new attitude went hand in hand not only with the desire for mobility, flexibility and change, but also with a new culture of inbuilt obsolescence.

Ettore Sottsass (born 1917)
Factotum bookshelves from the Alchimia Bau-Haus Collection, 1980

Wood, plastic laminate, h 230 cm, w 56 cm, d 48 cm
Manufacturer: Belux AG, Wohlen, Switzerland

Factotum was part of the First Bau-Haus Collection produced by the Alchimia group, which had its roots in the 'Radical Design' movement of the 1960s. In 1976, as a protest against the dictatorship of the good taste and the technologically oriented Functionalism of mass production, Alessandro Guerriero founded a design practice, which he named Alchimia and which he defined as a 'post-radical forum for discussion'. His partners in this enterprise were, among others, Alessandro Mendini, Andrea Branzi, Ettore Sottsass and Michele De Lucchi. Their fundamental aim was to replace the cold, functionalist aesthetic of the mass-produced objects associated with Italian 'Bel Design' with an emotional and sensual relationship between user and object. For this group, neither the possibility of serial production nor the ostensible function of an object were of significance; of prime consideration, on the other hand, were the expressive, wittily imaginative and ironic 'charisma' of the pieces produced. The name Alchimia stood for the programmatic intention of making gold out of things of little value. By means of loud colours and added decoration, design objects were to be created out of everyday items. Mendini, the theoretician of the group, went further in 're-decorating', and thus ironically questioning, well-known design classics with appliqué motifs, pennants and so on. 'There is no longer any originality,' he argued. 'The invention of new forms is being replaced by variety in decoration, patterns and surfaces. It is a case of design as re-design. Designing is now a process of decorating.'

Ettore Sottsass, on the other hand, took an entirely different path. As the pioneer of the anti-design movement in the 1960s, he had turned against the traditional dogmas of functionalism. His *Factotum* is an object created from basic stereometric forms coated with a laminate. He thereby secured an *entrée* to the living room for a material that, on account of its cheap image, had previously only been used in kitchens or in public places – bars, restaurants or waiting rooms. Items such as *Factotum* also achieved a significant intensification of expression through the combination of simple forms: this did much to encourage the emotional relationship postulated by Alchimia between user and object. Simultaneously, the connection between banality and irony, between historical citation, and a sense of fashion, fulfilled the need for aestheticizing art-objects that, through their limited editions, acquired the aura associated with the unique work of art. It was, however, precisely the proximity of these objects to works of art, in addition to the rather pessimistic intellectual approach of Mendini, that prompted Ettore Sottsass and several other designers to leave Alchimia in 1981 and to found Memphis, a less theoretically-bound design group and one more oriented to the practical. The designers of Memphis were less concerned with manifestos, performances, exhibitions or the production of programmatic individual pieces than with adopting and maintaining a positive attitude towards consumption, advertising, industry and daily life, for it was out of these that they derived much of their inspiration. Although these were expressly intended for serial production, they were not seen as destined for the mass market; rather, particular groups were targeted as potential customers. Both aesthetically and conceptually, Memphis products introduced a fundamentally new understanding of design.

Ettore Sottsass (born 1917)
***Sol* fruit bowl, 1982 / 83**

Multi-coloured blown glass, h 24 cm,
dia. (at rim) 29 cm, dia. (at base) c 11.5 cm
Manufacturer: Toso Vetri d'Arte, Murano, Italy

The Memphis group, founded in 1981, did not only design furniture and lamps but also textiles and objects made of glass, metal and ceramics. The *Sol* glass bowl is an example of how design principles derived from the qualities of specific materials were negated by Memphis, whose formal vocabulary is, in theory, applicable to any type of product. Decorative elements such as the blue triangles on the rim of the glass bowl might, for example, recur in a piece of furniture. Thus, design elements that are additive and independent from any particular material conquer a sphere traditionally associated with handicraft. Yet the objects designed by Sottsass have nothing to do with handicraft. Sottsass himself has described the production of his glass objects as 'a sort of revolution' in Murano, for the models were first of all produced as a series of individual components and only later assembled — theoretically speaking, each item could have been made in a mould.

Ettore Sottsass (born 1917)
***Ivory* side table, 1985**

Wood, laminated in multi-coloured plastic, crystal glass table top, h 100 cm, dia. 48 cm
Manufacturer: Memphis s.r.l., Pregnana Milanese, Italy

The *Ivory* table shows how the significance of the surface has changed. The use of plastic laminates led to the aesthetic reinstatement of this material in as far as 'a metaphor of vulgarity, poverty and bad taste' was stylized into a new vehicle for meaning. In the case of *Ivory*, decoration is no longer the opposite of function; decoration has become a structural component of the object. As Sottsass has observed: 'A Memphis table is decoration; [but now] structure and decoration are one.'

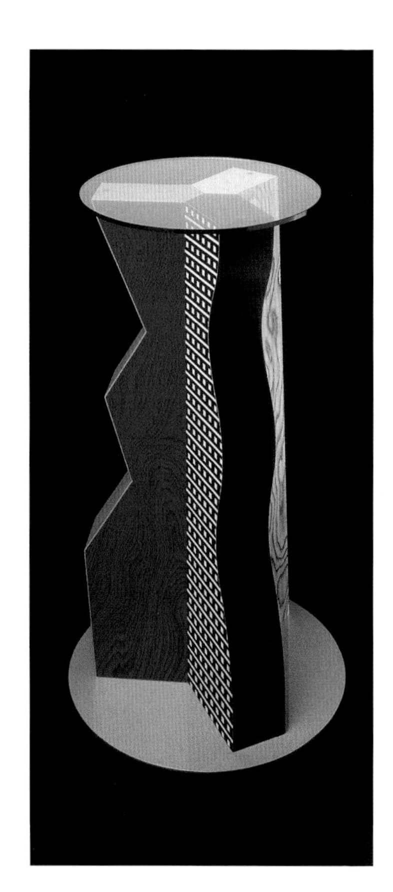

Laminates cannot only be applied to virtually any surface; they also offer the designer enormous scope and freedom. In the case of this table, Sottsass combines the imitation of a variety of types of wood with geometric patterning. In the case of other Memphis objects, the patterns were mostly derived through enlarging objects of everyday use, but also through inspiration derived from comic strips, films, the Punk movement, or kitsch. Often treated playfully, graphically witty and using loud colours, the design was intended to encourage spontaneous communication between object and spectator. The ungainly forms of many products recall those of toys; others take their inspiration from exotic cultures. They were a form of collage that made a principle out of chaos. Sottsass and his supporters saw this as a parallel to the non-commitment and obsessive mobility in the era of Post-Modernism.

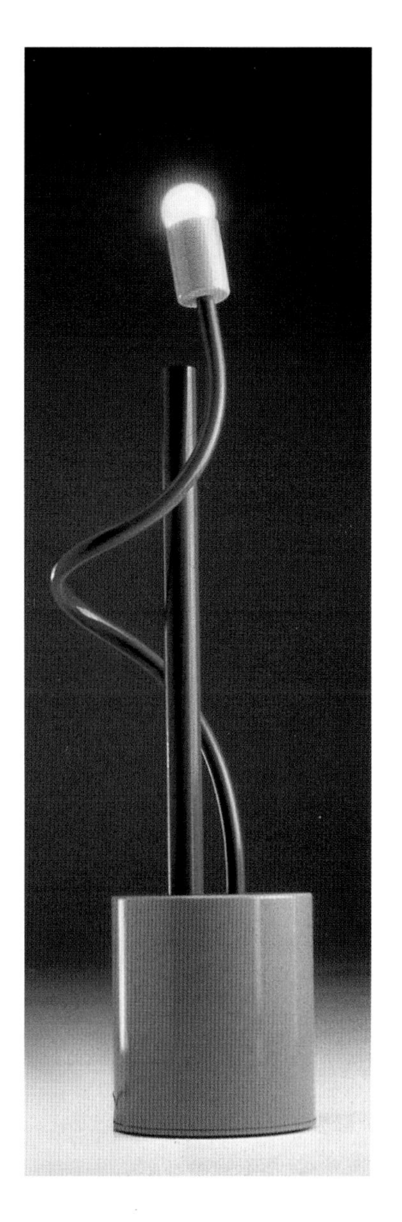

Michele De Lucchi (born 1951)
***Sinerpica* lamp from the Alchimia Bau-Haus Collection, 1979**

Metal varnished in various colours,
h 75 cm, dia. 17 cm
Manufacturer: Belux AG, Wohlen,
Switzerland

The table lamp *Sinerpica* was one of the first designs produced by Michele De Lucchi. Previously he had been engaged in architectural projects in the spirit of 'Radical Design'. De Lucchi transferred his energies almost directly from architecture to design when he got the chance to contribute to the first Bau-Haus Collection planned by the manufacturer Alchimia. The *Sinerpica* and a contemporary lamp, the *Speziale*, are testimony to De Lucchi's endeavour to transfer ideas developed in the realm of architecture into that of industrial design, and to link these with a new formal vocabularly. The shape of his lamp *Sinerpica*, for example, alluded to that of a potted plant climbing up a stick. In this respect, the *Sinerpica* already anticipates the associative formal language that was later to characterize the designs of Memphis.

Ingo Maurer (born 1932)
***One from the Heart* light object, 1989**

Partially nickel-plated metal, red and blue plastic, mirror glass, h 95 cm, max. w 40 cm
Manufacturer: Ingo Maurer GmbH, Munich, Germany

Ingo Maurer is regarded as one of the most important designers currently working with lighting. Since his first path-breaking design, the *Giant Bulb Clear* table lamp of 1966 (p. 102), he has gradually emerged as one of the most significant German designers and producers of lamps and lighting systems. His unconventional and playful approach to the medium of light is impossible to classify among any of the established tendencies in recent design; yet the visual and technical language of his objects evinces throughout an approach that is always original and sometimes idiosyncratic. For Maurer, the design of a lamp is not merely a question of intended function and candlepower; equally important is the question of the quality of the light and its relationship with the user. The *One from the Heart* lamp demonstrates that sense of the playful associated with Memphis, for this is not so much a lamp as a light object. As Maurer has said: 'I'm not proud of my design jokes. They simply occur, and strangely enough they have always occurred in connection with a wedding.'

Gaetano Pesce (born 1939)
***Green Street* chair, 1984**

Black polyester, chromium-plated metal,
h 94.5 cm, w 65 cm, d 55 cm
Manufacturer: Vitra AG, Basle, Switzerland

Gaetano Pesce, one of the most dazzling and enthusiastically experimental individuals in the 'Radical Design' movement, made his reputation above all with his innovative and intellectually penetrating projects for work with plastic. In 1993 he wrote of his *Green Street* chair: 'The *Green Street* chair involves two issues. One is the insecurity of this historical moment. We are living in an age when values are changing. The result is insecurity—insecurity about politics, religion, and culture, insecurity about the future of some minorities or ourselves, or about territories, or about the economic situation. I tried to represent the instability of our times with the *Green Street* chair, which gives when you sit on it. We incorrectly assume stability for a chair, but I want people to think about instability. The *Green Street* chair has structure but also movement. It is not as rigid as a traditional chair that gives you a feeling of security—you sit on it, you stay on it. The *Green Street* chair is a more flexible structure. It has eight very thin legs that allow a kind of movement.'

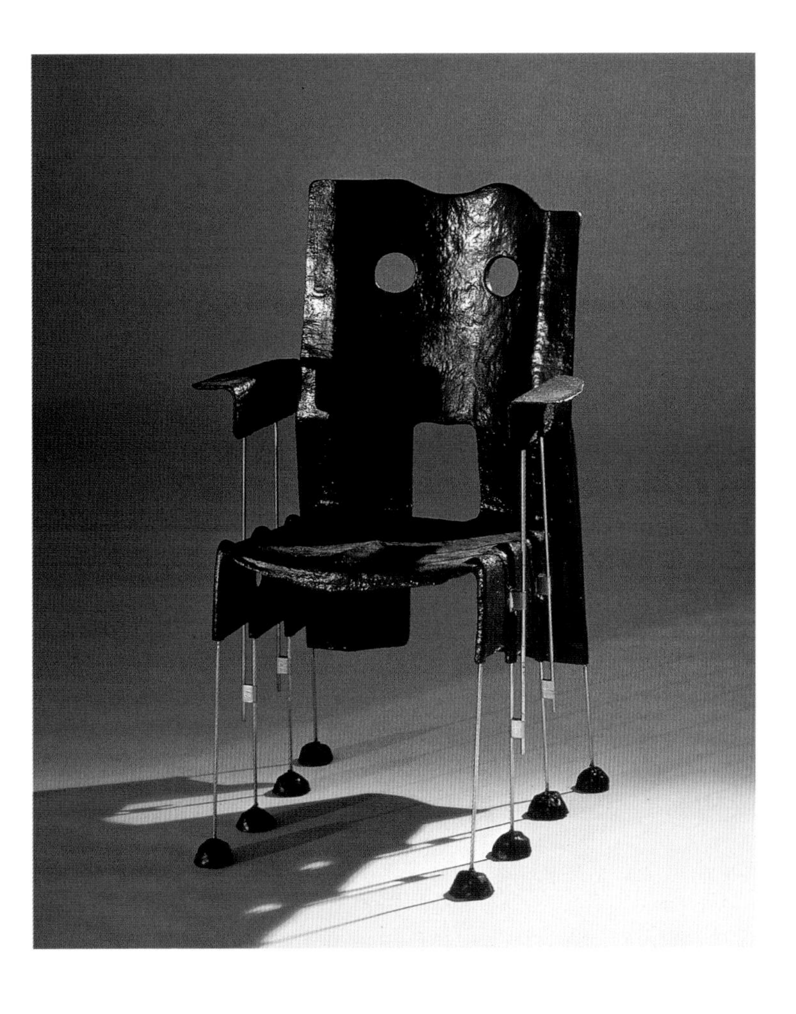

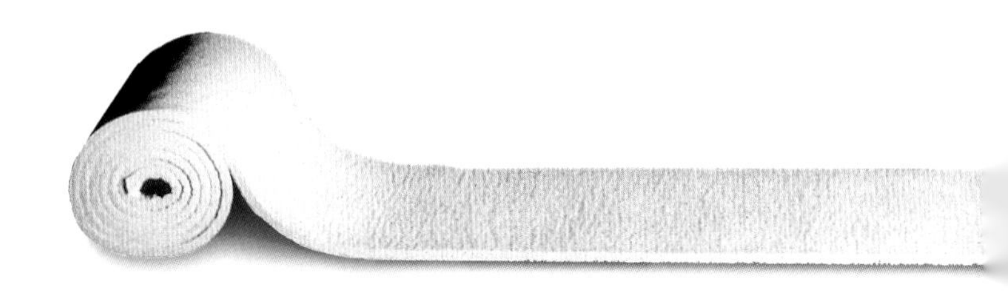

Rolf Sachs (born 1956)
***e geil* sleeping mat, 1993**

Grey felt, l 400 cm, w 60 cm, dia. (when rolled) 25 cm
Manufacturer: Rolf Sachs Function, London, England

The case of the *e geil* sleeping mat is paradigmatic of the transformation occurring in the work of the designer Rolf Sachs during the early 1990s. Sachs has himself commented on this: 'Earlier I was purely concerned with form as a purely aesthetic quality; but over the years I've tended more and more to a preoccupation with conceptual furniture – and with translating new thoughts and ideas into furniture.' Sachs constructs the objects he designs not out of shape-creating or form-determining elements; rather, he could almost be said to deconstruct them. He takes the essential function of each item as the starting point for his thoughts about it; in other words, he strips the object of anything that merely 'strikes a pose'. It is only then that a new entity emerges from the purely functional components that remain, their structures clearly revealed through offering to the user the chance to introduce changes to suit his or her own wishes and needs. In spite, or precisely because, of this, Sachs's elegantly reduced objects appear emphatically corporeal and real. The approach adopted by Sachs has also been applied to the question of the materials he has used in his more recent work. In contrast to many of his earlier pieces, for which he artfully adapted valuable materials, partially combined with expensive textiles, Sachs has now begun to work only with the simplest and most original materials, those that establish a compelling concord between form and function. Among these is felt.

Fauxpas
Rolled felt stool, 1992

Felt rolls, each with two metal bands, h 48 cm, dia. 36 cm
Manufacturer: Fauxpas GbR, Munich, Germany

The design group Fauxpas, established in 1985 and in existence until 1994, was founded by Herwig Huber (born 1965)

and Peter Grosshauser (born 1964). It first attracted attention with individual objects that its makers themselves described as 'usable sculpture'. In the late 1980s Fauxpas produced the first of several limited editions of domestic objects with designs that took a playful approach to both form and materials. In addition to steel, wood, plastic and stone, felt was sometimes employed. This is a material that in the 20th century had always been classified as 'cheap' and 'modest' until Joseph Beuys started to incorporate it in his work as an artist. But felt as an elemental textile did not come into its own in the realm of design. On account of its ability to store energy (in the form of warmth), it is connected with the simplest technologies for the preservation of life, and it appeals through its structure to our sense of touch. It was only in the late 1980s and early 1990s that designers started to use felt in its original form. In addition to the felt objects produced by Fauxpas, notable pieces were made by designers such as Gaetano Pesce, Marc Newson, Rolf Sachs and Jane Atfield. The rolled felt stool produced by Fauxpas is a simple but compelling solution for informal seating. Unproblematic and cheap to produce, simultaneously tough and soft, felt meets the demands of 'functional design', but at the same time breaks with the traditional material aesthetic of design on account of its semantic associations.

Heinz Landes (born 1961)
***Solid* chair, 1986**

Concrete, Monier iron,
h 117 cm, w 35.5 cm, d 44 cm
Manufacturer: Heinz Landes, Pforzheim, Germany

Heinz Landes is one of the most important representatives of the 'New German Design' that, in the early 1980s, deliberately unsettled many of the time-honoured notions still prevailing in this area. With furniture made of steel, concrete, rubber, metal sheeting and other unusual materials, with expressive shapes and experimental design processes, they succeeded in calling into question the functionalist design of the post-war era, originally associated with the College of Design in Ulm. Thomas Hauffe has written of this development: 'Experimental furniture, unique pieces and limited editions were produced, and every item questioned not only the concept of "function" but also the training received by designers. [Also called into question were] the constraints imposed by the production and distribution methods of a furniture industry that, despite a seemingly increasing diversification in the habits of consumers and users, still held fast to the dogma of mass production, and the resulting rectangular armchairs, boring corner units, pseudo-Historicist fitted cupboards and "rustic" three-piece suites.' Just as the concrete and steel of the *Solid* chair reflect the influence on design of an urban sub-culture, so its production methods break with conventional aesthetics.

Stiletto
***Consumer's Rest* armchair, 1983**

White zinc-plated metal,
h 100 cm, w 75.7 cm, d 68 cm
Manufacturer: Brüder Siegel GmbH + Co. KG, Leipheim, Germany

A further important tendency embraced by 'Neues Deutsches Design' is represented by Frank Schreiner (born 1959), who worked under the name Stiletto. His *Consumer's Rest* — which has become a trademark for this development — stands for the use of industrial semi-finished products and, as such, for what has been termed 'Readymade-Design'. By introducing some minor changes in the structure of a supermarket trolley, a chair is produced: an object from the hectic world of the consumer is transformed into a piece of furniture for the living room. The use of industrial semi-finished products in creating design objects is intended to provoke reflection on both the behaviour of the contemporary consumer and the character of domestic lifestyle. Schreiner / Stiletto has said of his furniture designs: 'They are intended to [be ...] clear in their construction, emphatically "real" through their direct association with industry, stable and solid, and suitable for serial production. It seemed to me that these conditions were most easily met if I used containers primarily intended for the daily circulation of consumer goods as my starting point in terms of materials [...]. "Re-design" has here less to do with recycling these with re-birthing.'

Philippe Starck (born 1949)
***Jim Nature* television set, 1993**

Pre-moulded sawdust-paste panels, grey-green plastic, h 37.5 cm, w 37.5 cm, d 39 cm
Manufacturer: Saba, Hanover, Germany

In 1992 the French entertainment electronics manufacturer Thomson, which also owned the trademarks Saba, Nordmende and Telefunken, wanted to commission the design of several Paris show rooms from Philippe Starck. It occurred to this designer that a space designed by him would only accentuate the bad design of Thomson products. Starck was, accordingly, appointed the company's Art Director. He assembled an international team of designers to work with him in radically redesigning the entire Thomson range. 'After I'd become completely annoyed at the sad grey and black plastic casing of the televisions, I was eventually able to convince them [the company] that there *were* alternatives. I took a material with which I was familiar and made a casing out of pre-moulded sawdust paste panels, which I glued together. *Jim Nature* was born. And because this television looked so different, it became a best-seller.'

Inflate (Nick Crosbie, Michael and Mark Sodeau)
Inflatable egg cup, 1995

Polyvinyl chloride (PVC), in lilac, pale blue, turquoise, yellow and orange,
h 5.5 cm, dia. 12 cm
Manufacturer: Inflate, England

The company name Inflate itself indicates the group's programme. Under the motto 'fun, functional and affordable', it produced a whole series of original and witty designs in welded PVC film: vases, fruit bowls, ashtrays, lamps, armchairs and so on. The inflatable egg cup is one of Inflate's best-known products – not least because, in 1997, the British weekend newspaper *The Observer* gave away a free egg-cup with its Easter edition. The success of Inflate has been the result of both the quality of its designs and the union of design and production, which allows for speedy and flexible operation.

Konstantin Grcic, Thomas Schulte and Matthias Dietz
Copylight wall light, design no. 61:
***On / Off Light*, 1993 / 94**
(Illustrated on back cover)

Zinc sheet, colourless and milky acrylic glass, plastic film in green, red and black,
h 30 cm, w 30 cm, d 9 cm
Manufacturer: Brainbox, Leverkusen, Germany

The idea for the *Copylight* wall light came from the two German designers Matthias Dietz and Thomas Schulte. They devised a flat lampshade out of two square panels of acrylic glass, between which a sheet of plastic was clamped. They then simply placed behind this a 25-watt lightbulb and added a switch. Numerous internationally active designers and artists were asked to submit designs to be copied on to the plastic film, with the result that a vast range of different lampshade designs was available to the consumer. The simple principle of copying any motif at all on to the plastic, and the uncomplicated

process of swapping one sheet for another, also implied an unlimited extension of the product. The Munich-based designer Konstantin Grcic (born 1965) also contributed to the project. His *On/Off* sheet, on account of its colouring and lettering, alludes to the workings of traffic lights and switches. It also draws on multi-functionality as the design principle that characterizes many of the objects he produced in the early 1990s, for example his combined clothes hanger and brush, his *red/green* lamp or his furniture for the manufacturer Classicon. Grcic's work also offers an ironic commentary on the concept of the functional in modern design, just as the *Copylight* questions the demand for 'originality'.

Ron Arad (born 1951)
***Rover Chair* two-seater, 1981**

Partially black-varnished metal, black leather, h 95 cm, w 150 cm, d 91 cm
Manufacturer: One Off Ltd., London, England

Ron Arad first studied at the Art Academy in Jerusalem before moving to London in 1973, where he continued his studies at the Association School of Architecture. In 1981 he founded 'One Off Ltd.' Arad concentrated on constructing furniture and, as such, could work independently of the wishes of potential customers. This also meant that designs were realized on a relatively low budget. As in the case of Stiletto's *Consumer's Rest* armchair, the *Rover Chair* designed by Ron Arad is one of the 'readymade' pieces of furniture that established a new direction in design in the early 1980s. Arad cultivated a determinedly pragmatic 'readymade' principle that, in its application, resulted in work that never appears static or stiff or even effortful. For his *Rover Chair* he combined two used Rover car seats with a curved metal frame and sleeves. He was intrigued by the mechanical function of these mounted 'found components' and much appreciated the saving of the design or production energy that would have been necessary to make these from scratch. *Rover Chair* represents an object for which virtually no reworking is required to the existing car-seats, reclaimed from a junk yard.

Masanori Umeda (born 1941)
***Getsuen* armchair, 1990**

Metal, green plastic, polyurethane foam-rubber, blue velvet, h 90 cm, seat h 43 cm, w 107 cm, d 90 cm
Manufacturer: Edra S.p.A., Perignano, Italy

After the designs made for Memphis in the early 1980s—including a bed in the shape of a boxing ring which captured worldwide attention—Masanori Umeda produced the work for which he is now best known: a chair designed in 1990 and manufactured by the Italian firm Edra. In addition to *Getsuen*, he also designed an armchair shaped like a rose with thorned feet, the bar stool *Shoshun* and the table *Anthurium*, in the shape of a waterlily leaf. In Umeda's view, the rise of Japan to become one of the leading industrialized nations and the resultant affluence have been responsible for the destruction of the Japanese landscape, its cultural inheritance and soul. In order to encourage the rediscovery of the roots of Japanese culture, in particular its deep harmony with landscape and the plant world, Umeda turned to motifs from nature and in particular to flowers. 'A chair entitled *Getsuen*, meaning "a moonlit garden," has the image of the Kikyo flower [a Chinese bellflower] secretly blooming in such a garden. *Kikyo* is one of my favorite graceful flowers [...]. [The] expression *ka-cho-fu-getsu*—meaning "flowers, birds, the wind and the moon"—is often quoted to show the Japanese sense of beauty [...] materially poor but spiritially rich.' With this allusion to nature Umeda further developed the aesthetic of the Flower Power and Pop Art of the 1960s, albeit in an entirely different context. He was also motivated by his desire to emphasize the contrast between contemporary Japan and the Japan of tradition.

Droog Design (Rody Graumans)
***85 Lamps* lamp, model dmd–08, 1993**

Light bulbs, metal sockets, cable,
h 100 cm, max. w 75 cm
Manufacturer: DMD, Voorburg, Netherlands
Donated by Ahrend GmbH & Co KG, Munich, Germany

In 1993 the art historian Renny Ramakers and the designer Gijs Bakker, presenting themselves as 'Droog Design', exhibited a selection of unconventional objects made by young Dutch designers at the Milan Furniture Fair. They created the Droog Design Foundation and selected those new designs best suited to their image and philosophy in terms of quality and content. In collaboration with the manufacturer DMD (Development, Manufacturing and Distribution) the selected designs were adapted and marketed. This is what happened with the lamp designed by Rody Graumans (born 1968), with its design determined entirely by its technical components: clamp, cable, sockets and lightbulbs. Graumans said: 'I'm not into that "less is more" stuff. I just work in lowly situations, like with an ordinary lightbulb, things that don't have much value. [...] You can't avoid using a lightbulb, it's always part of a lamp's construction.'

Droog Design (Tejo Remy)
You can't lay down your memories
chest of drawers, model dd–22, 1991

Wood (maple etc.), partially varnished or laminated, textile belt, h c 110 cm, w c 120 cm
Manufacturer: Droog Design, Amsterdam, Netherlands
Donated by Ahrend GmbH & Co KG, Munich, Germany

This piece of furniture designed by Tejo Remy (born 1960) formed part of his final examination in Utrecht. He took his inspiration from Robinson Crusoe, who — stranded on a remote island — was forced to make use of whatever he could find immediately around him. Remy, accordingly, salvaged the drawers from discarded cupboards, desks, refrigerators, ovens and so on, and then gave them new wooden frames. His chest of drawers consists, however, not only of re-used parts; through these it symbolizes an accumulation of memories: 'Each drawer carries its own memories and these are all jumbled up in your head. So the chest must be just as chaotic. The great thing about it is that it trains your memory. You have to remember exactly what went into which drawer.' The chest of drawers is one of the designs that assured the successful debut of Droog Design at the Milan Furniture Fair in 1993.

Tom Dixon (born 1959)
***Pylon* chair (prototype), 1990**

Blue-varnished metal,
h 127 cm, w 59.5 cm, d 62 cm
Manufacturer: Space, London, England

Tom Dixon is today regarded as one of the most influential English designers. Like Ron Arad, he initially made furniture out of scrap metal and other junk; then he turned to serial production. His *Pylon* series of tables and chairs occupies a position between these two extremes, being made out of thin metal wire. Despite their extreme lightness, these objects are in fact tremendously stable. The *Pylon* series evinces Dixon's marked interest in materials and in advanced manufacturing processes.

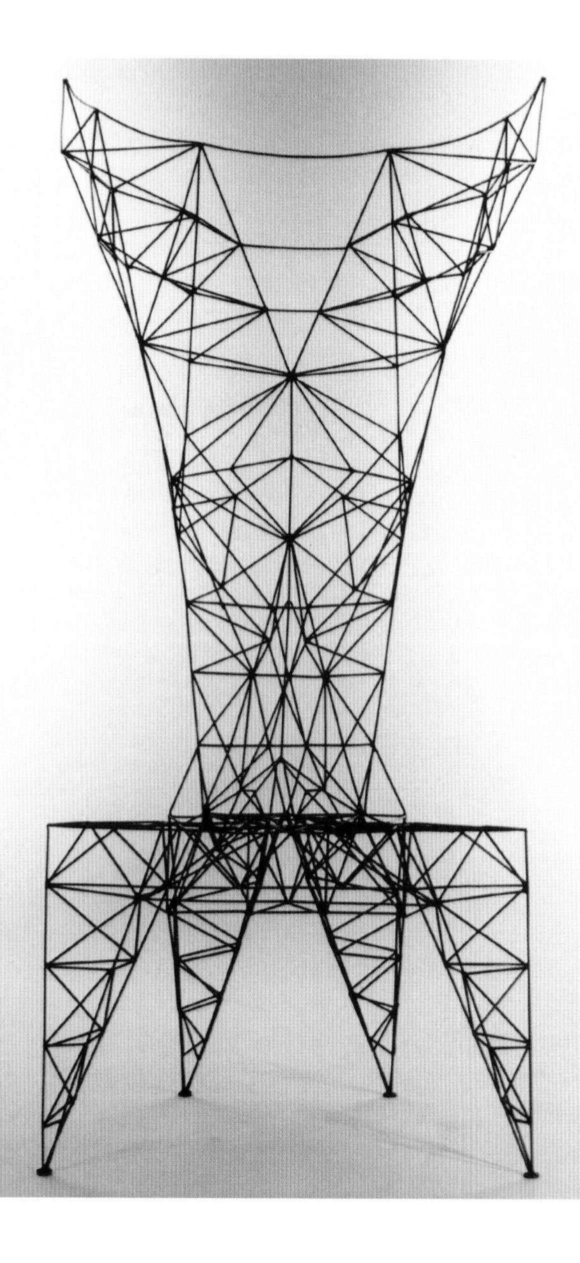

Jonathan Ive (Apple Design Group)
***iMac* computer, 1998**

Translucent white and blueish-green plastic,
h 39.5 cm, w 38 cm, d 44 cm
Manufacturer: Apple Computer Inc., USA

The *iMac* computer represents not only the enormous upheaval within the world of computing brought about by the increasing importance of the Internet, but also the related transformation in the structure of society in the late 20th century. Like the first Apple Macintosh computers, emphasis is placed both on the now legendary user-friendliness associated with these machines, and on the integration of various components and technologies. Of particular importance, however, is the unusual design of the casing: shape, colour and material introduce a surprisingly new element into the sad, predominantly grey world of the PC. The ovoid form of the casing and the coloured semi-transparent plastic used for this underline, moreover, the promotion of the *iMac* as an 'intelligent object' that will be able to adapt to and profit from new technological developments. Even the smallest details, therefore, were considered in relation to the notion of global communication: from the design of the interior and the shape of the reinforced ribbed structure to the lettering or the system of packaging. This also explains the use of semi-transparent coloured plastic, for by this means the otherwise hidden interior becomes visible and, in this respect, an embodiment of advanced technology is demystified. Every element in the design speaks a clear, easily comprehensible language. The handle suggests mobility and lightness, there is no tangle of cables at the back, peripherals can be attached by means of a standard plug. Every component in the system (right down to the keyboard and the mouse) is informed by a unified, integrated design concept, and this also relates to price, computing power and the attached software package, which is intended to simplify access to the Internet.

Index

Aarnio, Eero 93, 104
Angermann, Peter 64
Antes, Horst 51
Arad, Ron 120
Armando 52

Balkenhol, Stephan 49
Baselitz, Georg 53
Beltzig, Günter 105
Beuys, Joseph 40
Bijl, Guillaume 66

Casati, Cesare 100
Charbonneaux, Philippe 84
Cocteau, Jean 89

De Lucchi, Michele 111
Delvoye, Wim 65
Dietz, Matthias 119
Dimitrijević, Braco 58
Dixon, Tom 124
Drocco, Guido 92
Droog Design 122, 123

Eames, Charles und Ray 78
Eppich, Egon 36

Fauxpas 114
Federle, Helmut 55
Fruhtrunk, Günter 32
Fuller, Paul 76

Ghyczy, Peter 98
Gilardi, Piero 96
Graevenitz, Gerhard 33
Graubner, Gotthard 31
Grcic, Konstantin 119
Gugelot, Hans 89
Gursky, Andreas 68

Heidenreich, Fritz 89
Honert, Martin 67
Horn, Roni 71

Inflate 118
Ive, Jonathan 125

Jacobsen, Arne 80, 81

Kagan, Vladimir 79
Kantor, Tadeusz 24
Kern, Stephan 46
Kiecol, Hubert 48
King, Perry A. 106
Knaupp, Werner 50
Knifer, Julije 37
Kolář, Jiři 22, 23
Koppel, Henning 82
Kosuth, Joseph 59
Kuehn, Gary 42

Landes, Heinz 116
Lébovici, Yonel 102, 103
Leccia, Ange 63
Lindner, Richard 20, 21
Lomazzi, Paolo 107
Long, Richard 45
Lucini, Ennio 101

Maciunas, George 41
Mangiarotti, Angelo 87
Marotta, Gino 100
Maurer, Dora 34
Maurer, Ingo 102, 112
McCaslin, Matthew 60
Mello, Franco 92
Millares, Manolo 27
Möbus, Christiane 62
Mollino, Carlo 85
Morassutti, Bruno 87
Morellet, François 38

Noguchi, Isamu 79

Paik, Nam June 61
Panton, Verner 88
Parigi, Vittorio 99
Pas, Jonathan de 107
Penck, A.R. 54
Pesce, Gaetano 113
Pfahler, Georg Karl 35
Piene, Otto 28
Polke, Sigmar 56
Ponzio, Emanuele 100
Porsche, Ferdinand 74
Prina, Nani 99

Rams, Dieter 89
Rancillac, Bernard 98
Rheinsberg, Raffael 47
Riley, Bridget 30
Ruff, Thomas 69
Ruthenbeck, Reiner 44

Sachs, Rolf 114
Sarpaneva, Timo 82
Schoonhoven, Jan 29
Schulte, Thomas 119
Smith, Leon Polk 39
Sonnier, Keith 43
Sottsass, Ettore 106, 108, 109, 110
Starck, Philippe 118
Stiletto 117
Studio 65 97
Stupica, Gabrijel 25

Trockel, Rosemarie 57

Umeda, Masanori 121
Urbino, Donato d' 107

Vostell, Wolf 26

Wagenfeld, Wilhelm 86
Warhol, Andy 90

Zaugg, Rémy 70

Front cover: Richard Lindner, Telephone, 1966 (see p. 21)
Back cover: Konstantin Grcic, Thomas Schulte and Matthias Dietz, Copylight wall light, design no. 61: *On/Off Light*, 1993/94 (see p. 119)

Photo credits:
pp. 4/5, 7, 13, 14: Neues Museum in Nuremberg (Margherita Spiluttini); p. 8: Bischof & Broel KG, Nuremberg ; pp. 11, 18/19, 22, 31, 33–35, 38–51, 56–63, 65–67, 70, 71: Neues Museum in Nuremberg (Annette Kradisch); p. 17: Udo Meinel, Berlin; pp. 20, 21, 23–30, 32, 36, 37, 52–55, 64, 68, 69: Neues Museum in Nuremberg (Kurt Paulus et al); pp. 72, 73: Klaus Frahm, Hamburg; pp. 74, 75: Continental Teves, Frankfurt; pp. 76, 77 top, 79, 81, 83–88, 89 top, 93–95, 98–101, 105, 106 bottom, 107, 115: Die Neue Sammlung (Angela Bröhan).
All other illustrations are from the archives of the Neue Sammlung or have been provided by the respective manufacturer or designer.

Die Deutsche Bibliothek – CIP Einheitsaufnahme
Neues Museum Nuremberg – Munich ; London ; New York: Prestel, 2000 (Prestel Museum Guide)
ISBN 3-7913-2318-0

Prestel Verlag
Mandlstrasse 26, 80802 Munich, Germany
Tel. (089) 38 17 09–0, fax (089) 38 17 09–35;
4 Bloomsbury Place, London WC1A 2QA
Tel. (0171) 3235004, fax (0171) 6368004;
16 West 22nd Street, New York, NY 10010, USA
Tel. (212) 627–8199, fax (212) 627–9866

Authors:
Lucius Grisebach (LG)
Thomas Heyden (TH)
Melitta Kliege (MK)
Birgit Suk (BS)
Text on pp. 74–125 by Josef Straßer
German edition edited by Thomas Heyden and Josef Straßer

Translated from the German and edited by Elizabeth Clegg, London
Designed and typeset by WIGEL, Munich
Printed and bound by Passavia Druckservice GmbH, Passau

Printed in Germany on acid-free paper
ISBN 3-7913-2318-0